Praise for *Coach*

'I'm looking forward to using this book to teach leadership to university students as well as with executives. It's great that you can read it from start to finish as well as dig in when you have a specific problem.'
Lina Sors Emilsson, ReSors Technology AB, Sweden and Uppsala University

'Most coaching books *tell* you how to coach. This one *shows* you.'
Paul Smith, bestselling author, *Lead with a Story* and *The 10 Stories Great Leaders Tell*

'A novel and useful way to think about coaching. Relevant to every leader.'
Sheelagh Whitaker, Global NED; author, *Evaline: A Feminist's Tale*

'Great companies need great managers who see it as their responsibility to bring out the potential and performance of their people. Key to this is the ability to coach in the moment, or on-the-go within the context of the job. Phil and Jenny's book, *Coaching On the Go*, brings this to life.'
John Millea, Director People Development, SAP

'A completely useable, practical guide to developing successful coaching techniques in order to be a more effective leader.'
Blair Illingworth, CEO Stirling Plc

'If you are a busy leader, wanting to increase your effectiveness and impact, this book helps equip you with techniques to do just that. It is easy to digest and keeps it simple, helping you to ask more empowering questions to become a more effective leader.'
Karena Freeman, Executive Partner, Global Research and Advisory Firm

'The skills you need to coach are clearly explained with lots of great ideas to put them into practice.'
Subhan Iswahyudi, B2B Sales Coach; Leadership Development Expert; Faculty Member, Telkom Indonesia Corporate University

'This fun and well-informed manual helps to make practical coaching more accessible to everyone.'
Matt Nixon, CEO coach; former Vice President, OE, Shell

'Wow! What a refreshing approach to help someone learn how to use a coaching style to bring the best out of people in a most human and natural way!'
Lester Coupland, Executive Development Director, Cranfield University

'I love this book. Jenny and Phil show you how all leaders can improve their coaching skills. Follow their simple steps wherever you are on the journey and you will be a more successful leader.'
Andrew Hall, Partner, Haywood Mann

Coaching On the Go

Pearson

At Pearson, we have a simple mission: to help people make more of their lives through learning.

We combine innovative learning technology with trusted content and educational expertise to provide engaging and effective learning experiences that serve people wherever and whenever they are learning.

From classroom to boardroom, our curriculum materials, digital learning tools and testing programmes help to educate millions of people worldwide – more than any other private enterprise.

Every day our work helps learning flourish, and wherever learning flourishes, so do people.

To learn more, please visit us at **www.pearson.com/uk**

Coaching On the Go

How to lead your team effectively in 10 minutes a day

Phil Renshaw and Jenny Robinson

 Pearson

Harlow, England • London • New York • Boston • San Francisco • Toronto • Sydney
Dubai • Singapore • Hong Kong • Tokyo • Seoul • Taipei • New Delhi
Cape Town • São Paulo • Mexico City • Madrid • Amsterdam • Munich • Paris • Milan

PEARSON EDUCATION LIMITED
KAO Two
KAO Park
Harlow
CM17 9SR
United Kingdom
Tel: +44 (0)1279 623623
Web: www.pearson.com/uk

First edition published 2019 (print and electronic)

ISBN: 978-1-292-26791-3 (print)
       978-1-292-26792-0 (PDF)
       978-1-292-26793-7 (ePub)

British Library Cataloguing-in-Publication Data
A catalogue record for the print edition is available from the British Library

Library of Congress Cataloging-in-Publication Data
A catalog record for the print edition is available from the Library of Congress

10 9 8 7 6 5 4 3 2 1

23 22 21 20 19

Cover design by Two Associates

Print edition typeset in 9.5/13pt Mundo Sans by SPi Global
Printed by Ashford Colour Press Ltd, Gosport

NOTE THAT ANY PAGE CROSS REFERENCES REFER TO THE PRINT EDITION

**How to lead your team
effectively in 10 minutes a day**

COACHING
ON THE GO

**PHIL RENSHAW
JENNY ROBINSON**

Contents

About the authors

We could not imagine writing plain bios about ourselves, so we have cheated and written about each other...

What Jenny says about Phil:

He is definitely not a cliché. After 20 years as a classic finance guy (yes, his childhood ambition was to be a banker!), Phil suddenly realised that it wasn't all about the money – it's all about the people! Those 'numbers' only get you so far. When I heard this story and he talked about writing together, I couldn't wait.

Phil was a successful international banker for nearly ten years and fortunate enough to live and work in London, New York and Sydney. Thereafter, he joined EDS (a global IT outsourcer) where he continued his finance career, leading the EMEA Treasury/Corporate Finance teams and then onto Finance Director positions in the UK.

In the midst of all that success, his first epiphany was that he didn't want to be an FD. And his second epiphany was that he did want to work with developing people. It was a natural choice for him to become a coach. I found our writing collaboration completely exhilarating. Phil's sharp wit and intellect shone throughout.

What Phil says about Jenny:

Jenny has heaps of commercial experience having built and run several successful companies. The commercial radio station she co-established as an 18 year old in New Zealand continues to this day! As an Equity Partner in Towers Perrin, a global Actuarial, HR and Change Consulting Firm, she forged a truly international career with clients in Asia, Europe, America and Africa.

Appropriately for *Coaching On-the-Go*, Jenny has a private Pilot's licence and has had a dodgy landing – you'll see that our book takes liberties with this. But she says, the fear was real.

While she had a seemingly magical early career, a tragedy left Jenny poleaxed for almost a year. Rehabilitation came through the madness of alpaca farming and mindfulness! She now guides others through leadership development, coaching and mentoring, alongside a constant drive to keep learning – especially about leadership. With work taking her all over the world with clients big and small, she was the perfect person to write this book with. I enjoyed every moment. And I expect you will too.

Together, *we have extensive experience of the highs and lows in life, of coaching and supporting others and the belief that we can all learn the skills of coaching to improve our leadership capabilities. Please enjoy reading our book. And if you want to know more about our stories go to* www. coachingonthego.co.uk.

Dedications

Many people have been influential in our personal coaching journeys. We want to take a moment to acknowledge them as they are great coaches and leaders, still with much to offer – to you and to us.

For Phil:

- Deryn Holland – a brilliant coach, supervisor and trainer from whom I have learned a great deal. Many of her techniques and ideas are reflected in this book. A critical influencer and friend on my journey.

- Sandy Malloy – key to my personal transition into becoming a coach. And, as her husband Pete likes to joke, she taught me (a hackneyed finance guy, comfortable with numbers and facts) the power of the question 'And how does that make you feel?'

- My long-standing European coach mentoring/supervision group. In alphabetical order the core members are José de Sousa, Karena Freeman, John Hardwick, Steve Hobbs, Bettina Kapp, Lutz Lemmer and Christel Meyer. Together, in our monthly calls, we have a wonderful group for testing and learning our skills. Thank you all.

For Jenny:

- Dr Terry Morgan (RIP) – Terry resisted any dogma in coaching training, believing that this can be a truly quirky and individual undertaking. His recognition that all of life and all relationships could be the site of coaching inspired me to look beyond the usual.

- Jessica McNicholas – simply the best coach I have ever had the pleasure of watching at work. Her values of serving the client have made her brave beyond belief and an inspiration to anyone who wants to be astoundingly transformational.

Acknowledgements

We want to highlight two people who have been very big supporters and instrumental in getting this book finished:

- Caroline Jayne Ellis – our truly wonderful designer. Her ideas for the artwork in this book really inspired us on our journey. If anyone needs any design work for frankly anything, Caroline should be your first choice.

- Mark Ellis, Head of Operations, OpenText (and yes, he and Caroline are married). Mark has been a passionate supporter of our idea and been a great help given his own publishing journey (check out Digitox – How to find a Healthy Balance for your Family's Digital Diet). As an expert in cultural change, leadership development and a self-expressed 'data geek' he's given thoughtful advice, practical help and been happy to invite us into his network.

Publisher's acknowledgements

Text Credits:

42 Ken Blanchard: Ken Blanchard **62 Hanford Lennox Gordon:** Hanford Lennox Gordon **140 Albert Einstein Archives:** Albert Einstein **156 Pearson Education:** Hersey, P., & Blanchard, K. H. Management of organization behavior: Utilizing human resources. 3rd ed. Englewood Cliffs, N. J.: Prentice Hall, Inc. 1977 **159 University of California Western Training Lab:** Luft, J. & Ingham, H. 1955. The Johari window: A graphic model for interpersonal relations, University of California Western Training Lab

Photo Credit:

ix Carola Moon: Carola Moon **x B Cientanni:** B Cientanni

Introduction

We met in a lecture theatre at Cranfield School of Management in the UK as we started out on our PhDs in 2015. It was Phil's idea to write a book and have a parable as a central spine to hold the main teaching points, and as Cranfield is the only university we know of that has its own airfield for Pilot training, it was a small step from Phil's original idea to a story about a global airline.

The idea fired Jenny's enthusiasm and fuelled some of the offshoots of the book. Like all great partnerships, about two years on, neither of us can actually remember who has contributed what and we really don't care. From one great book idea many other ideas have been spawned and we now offer coaching workshops, keynote presentations and blogs.

In 2018, in collaboration with Cranfield School of Management, we started a podcast where leaders with practical examples of using *Coaching On-the-Go* tell their stories and inspire others to follow in their footsteps. We both believe, and we share this with other leaders who collaborate with us, that great leaders are made, not born, and central to this belief is that skills can be taught.

Coaching On-the-Go has an emancipatory objective to make coaching skills available to any leader who has ten minutes a day to invest in themselves and the people they work with.

Part 1

About this book

Welcome on board

There is an ever-increasing need for leading and coaching skills to be united because evidence shows that leaders who coach their team members are most likely to engender behaviour that is consistent with the team's objectives. If you are a leader, or an aspiring leader, we want to show you how to learn and use coaching skills in a manner consistent with your working life – *On-the-Go*.

That is what this book delivers. Ten-minute chapters. Bite-sized sections with activities you can quickly practise. Short sections you can read and reflect on during your commute and sections you can read in any order because each one is self-contained. In each chapter we explain a key component of the coaching skillset. Why it is important, when to use it and what to expect. In many cases the exercises we offer to develop these skills are designed to help you notice the positive impacts of coaching skills on yourself as well as the impact on others. Both are powerful.

Leaders can use coaching skills with their team members, colleagues, clients – and pretty much everyone. Leaders know their people best, the context in which they work and the challenges they face, so working with people using coaching is a natural adjunct to other leadership skills.

Our premise is simple. Business life today is a continuously messy activity. Coaching opportunities happen at unpredictable times and not at the behest of a coach's presence or a pre-agreed meeting. Leaders who are closest to the action are best placed to seize the coaching opportunity. That's you. (Unless you are a professional coach – in which case, you might already know many of these skills, but we hope you discover and try out others that you don't know. And even copy our techniques. By the way, thanks for buying the book.)

Whether you're a leader or a coach, we give you short activities to develop the skills to seize the opportunities that business life presents to you. Just one word of warning – if you think this stuff is obvious, in our experience people who pour scorn on these skills actually don't coach – or won't coach. So before you get sniffy about this, test yourself, stretch yourself. It may be obvious but that doesn't make it easy. That's our point.

Why use an airline to make the point?

To illustrate the skills of coaching and to draw attention to how they occur all the time in normal working life, we tell a story that runs through the main flight. Our story follows the trials and tribulations of a team working at a fictional global airline.

The choice of an airline to place our story is simply because we think most people can understand the context within which they work, which makes it easier to understand and relate to what is happening. Global airlines face many of the same challenges as other global businesses: cost/service considerations; finding, keeping and developing global talent; complex supply chains; fast pace of change and innovation; fierce competition.

Neither of us have specialist knowledge of the airline industry, so please accept our humble apologies if we have inadvertently misrepresented anything in our fictional scenes.

This airline theme is intended to keep things clear and bring a smile or two along the way. Mostly, it is here to make sure that our teaching points are accessible and clearly relate to business situations that you will recognise. We are firm believers that we can enjoy the developmental and learning journey whatever career stage we are at. Work should be fun, and this book aims to follow that maxim.

In keeping with the airline theme and our promise to make this an *On-the-Go* book, we have separate sections with distinct aims and we have used the icons shown on the left to help you find the different sections quickly.

Icons	Sections
✈ FAST TRACK ⟫	A navigation section offers the 'Fast Track' to help you quickly identify typical scenarios and some fast, effective next steps.

Icons	Sections
	Part 2: The main flight. This is where you will find the core coaching skills. The airline story develops in each chapter to help demonstrate the issues. Each chapter should take you ten minutes to read and understand, and provide many activities to practise.
	At the end of each chapter we offer a series of straightforward activities for you to practise the coaching skill we've explained. These may be the best place to start for you if you are new to the ideas or perhaps more challenged by the ideas. In flying terms, these equate to being good at the **basics** – *Flying Straight and Level*. An odd thing about several coaching skills is that they sound like something you've known how to do for years. For example, you might wonder what you have to learn about listening, given that most of us have been doing it since birth. We think these skills are often not as easy as they might sound, and hence practising these basics is very valuable.
	At the end of each chapter we also offer a series of more **challenging** activities for you to develop the coaching skills we've been exploring to a greater level. These activities presume you've mastered the basics. Naturally, with a flying theme, these are consistent with aerial acrobatics – *Looping the Loop*. You can start with these if you feel comfortable enough not to practise the basics, although we'd recommend reading the *Flying Straight and Level* options as they may be useful in helping you prepare.

Icons	Sections
	Part 3: The Pilot's manual. This allows you to develop your expertise even further by taking a deeper dive into the skills of coaching. Part 2 is critical to your coaching skills as a leader and in this third part we simply offer you more. Using coaching models and leadership theory, we offer new activities and ideas to develop your coaching prowess. These include activities that you might undertake with colleagues, team members or others around you. This works on the same principles as the rest of the book where everything is in ten-minute sections. We also share the key coaching competences as described by the main global coaching professional bodies.

Wherever you start, all the learning chunks are bite-sized (or flight-sized if you want to stick with our aeronautical theme), and for most of us that means commute-sized. Ten minutes is all it takes to get something you can use when you arrive at your office. If you happen to be on a longer journey, you can simply add several ten-minute sections together.

We've written this book so that it accommodates a number of different learning styles so you can find a way that most suits you. This follows the principle of coaching that every individual learns in their own way. You can dip in and out in any order that supports your needs. If you've just had a meeting that did not go as planned, you can dip into the relevant chapters of this book on your commute home to see what you might do differently next time. If a member of your team seems stuck on a project, you can read how to get them unstuck as you eat your lunch. We also offer two other routes that warrant further explanation.

First, if you just want to read the central concepts in one sitting and you enjoy learning through storytelling, you can read the story set in 11 scenes embedded into the chapters in Part 2. But let's be frank, some people do not relate to the use of a parable or fictional stories – and if this is you, then ignore the parable completely. However, if you read the parable from beginning to end, you will follow the story of our fictional team which we use to illustrate certain situations. The story is based around our experiences as coaches and business leaders and you can eavesdrop on this team as they go from a tricky beginning to a (spoiler alert) happy ending.

The story used to illustrate the ideas in this book is based around the flight crew of an airline. Here's a cast list of the main characters.

Throughout the story we have a narrator to help, and as you might expect with our flying theme, he's an air traffic controller (ATC). He can see the bigger picture and guide us through the issues.

The crew of UsFlyHiPo

Prya is the chief Pilot and overall team leader for our flight crew. She's a modern-day paragon of leadership virtue.

Caroline is currently first officer and hoping for a promotion to captain. Although she is a very capable Pilot, she has some rough edges that prevent her contributing fully.

FC is the boss we all want to have. He is the flight crew's leader on the ground and believes in developing his team. He invests in their growth and shows them clearly what it takes to be successful. No one remembers his real name so he's known by all as FC.

Asif shares the privilege of flying up front with Prya and Caroline. He's not far behind Caroline waiting for promotion and she's aware that he is snapping at her heels.

Tomacz is a canny and supremely professional member of the crew. He has high IQ and Emotional Intelligence (known as EQ) and skilfully won't suffer fools gladly. Equally skilfully, he tells it like it is and he's no respecter of rank.

Shilpa is the person that every team needs. Someone to go to for a listening ear, empathy and sound advice. Although she is frazzled, she knows how to attend to the needs of others.

Anja is the youngest member of the team. Completely unconcerned with the team dynamics, she's joined the airline to see the world, spend as many hours as possible pool-side before flying to the next exotic location for more fun.

Henrik has a razor-sharp intelligence hidden behind a slight tendency to do as little as possible. Henrik is up for a good time, but shirks hard work. The team don't resent him at all, because his humour and demeanour are so endearing.

Kristoff has a tendency towards too much detail. He is highly strung and believes that it is his perfectionism that keeps this crew at the top of their game. But you know what, he might be partially right.

The competition

JumboJumbo, a lower cost airline with even lower standards.

Your authors

Phil and Jenny. We couldn't resist putting ourselves in the book, but not in the main story. But please don't forget that while our friends above are fictional, we're real people. We're in the book because we think we have valuable experiences to share that illuminate a few key points. The stories we tell are all true – anonymised as you would expect.

Reading the story in one go will take you no more than 30 minutes. Reflecting on what you can learn from it will take much longer.

✈ FAST TRACK ❯ Alternatively, when you do not have time to read the whole book, you can skip the queues and use the Fast Track guide which provides a look up menu on what to do when faced with an immediate issue. This is a unique feature of this book. It addresses your immediate needs to help you find a potential way forward in ten minutes.

The content does not follow some perfect flight-path. Life is not like that and neither is this book. To practise the skills in each chapter you do not have to have practised those in the preceding chapters. Nonetheless, the skills of coaching are highly inter-related. As you improve in one area, that will impact positively on your skills in another. Be prepared to duck and dive.

Whichever way you read through this book, we have one requirement – that you read the Safety Briefing first, which is at the end of this section. There we draw your attention to some critical and potentially challenging issues which need to be in your mind whenever you are coaching.

What is coaching?

Our guess is that you chose this book because you have an interest in the promise we make on the cover. But what is coaching and why are we excited to share these skills with you? The essence of coaching is a belief that people can find their own solutions to the challenges they face and that they can be energised by the growth and development that these challenges provide.

Most of us know coaching from sport where the coach is helping an athlete to be better, to jump higher, swim faster or score more goals. The coach can see the mistakes the athlete keeps making, they can see their natural abilities and limitations. Through coaching, the athlete becomes more accomplished. There are many parallels with this type of coaching and the things we discuss in this book.

As our focus is coaching in business, let us provide a simple definition that works for us: **Through coaching, people find solutions that work for them**. You may not think the solution would work for you, but the critical feature is that people think it will work for them and consequently they will be motivated to test out their solution. A variety of skills, each of which has value and impact in its own right, such as better listening, combine to create an effective coach. This book will teach you these skills.

SOME KEY TERMS

Throughout the management and executive coaching profession, the person coaching is referred to as the **coach** and the person they are working with as the **coachee**. Even if you coach your boss or your boss's boss we refer to them this way. Similarly, **mentor** and **mentee** are the person steering the process of mentoring and the receiver of the mentoring. (See below for a definition of mentoring and its distinction from coaching.)

In many cases when you are practising the skills in this book, or when we are describing the component techniques of coaching, you may not declare to someone that you are actively using coaching skills with them. There is no time. It's happening in the moment and you may be using one component skill rather than the full set. You are simply taking a *coaching approach.* This is especially relevant in those brief moments when you think how

▶

best you can help move an issue forward – by asking questions (a coaching style) or telling them (a directive leadership style).

Whether it is or is not a declared coaching conversation, for the sake of simplicity we refer to the other person in this dialogue as the coachee. This reduces long phrases like 'the person with whom you are using this coaching skill'. Our assumption through-out the book is that you are acting as the coach.

Why is this book different?

Let's face it, if you haven't noticed already there are lots of books out there on coaching. Even more on leadership and because leading is seen as vital for business success the airport stores are full of these books. So, what's different about this book?

There is a tendency for most authors to assume that coaching is a formal interaction with a professional who has a pre-arranged conversation (face to face or virtual) with another person. These conversations are sched-uled in advance and often rely on an external coach who has undertaken a professional qualification in coaching and learnt certain skills.

In contrast, we advocate that leaders have the opportunity, if not the obligation, to use coaching skills in their day-to-day working life to max-imise their own effectiveness and the effectiveness of their teams, col-leagues and even their bosses. This happens *On-the-Go* or in the moment, not in some pre-ordained 'Let's sit down while I coach you' moment. Indeed, when using coaching skills with your peers or bosses you are pretty unlikely to declare that you are coaching – you are simply using those skills.

This book gives you access to those coaching skills in a way you can both learn *On-the-Go*, practise *On-the-Go* and become effective *On-the-Go*.

What's the evidence for coaching as an effective leadership skill?

Advances in neuroscience are now able to give us insight into effective leadership. Although leadership is often associated with making big decisions or good choices, in practice much of the work of leadership is focused on relationships. Every leader knows how important relationships are to their effectiveness. Now science is confirming that the neurological pathways that light up in brain scans differ according to different leadership styles.

As humans we are social creatures, and intuitively we know that connectivity lies at the heart of leadership. Our social orientation is easily understood from an evolutionary psychology perspective. In cave-dwelling days our survival as individuals relied on our ability to fit in and live in harmony in our community. Rejection from the tribe was life-threatening. While that was true in pre-historic times, not much has changed at a biological level in the intervening millennia. The brain's regions that monitor pro-social behaviour remain deeply embedded even in twenty-first-century humans.

These insights explain other findings by researchers who use MRI scanners to measure brain activity. They have observed that research participants recalling leaders who work in a way that is inclusive and respectful activate brain regions that are typically used for creativity and innovative problem-solving. Such leaders provide sufficient safety for others to 'come off alert' and to engage fully using their full cognitive capacity.

Our conjecture is that these leaders who coach allow people to bring the best of themselves to work. They actively build relationships of trust which allow individuals to gain new perspectives on themselves and their work situation.

Getting the best out of people is now understood neurologically as well as psychologically. Coaching provides the best leadership style we have, based on good scientific evidence.

When is a leader acting as a coach?

Our focus is leadership in business and this also includes leadership of the self. In the following table we offer some broad, distinguishing features of leading versus coaching, as we see them.

Leading mode	Coaching mode
• Leaders provide direction so that everyone has a sense of where they're going and how they fit in. • Leaders make decisions, often these decisions have been passed upwards because they are complex and interconnected. Leaders take decisions others can't make. • Leaders work to get people aligned and pulling in the same direction and committed to the overall vision. • Leaders set priorities.	• Helping individuals to realise how much they are capable of achieving. Supporting them to achieve this, and showing them where they are overreaching themselves, or where they have limitations. • Clarifying with individuals their personal and professional development goals. • Giving feedback in service to an individual's achievement of their desired development goals. • Offering, where appropriate, ideas and experiences which people may choose to model. • Supporting individuals as they try new things and take personal steps to meet their desired goals.

It is useful to draw attention to the fact that some people would argue that these two modes present a false dichotomy and that many leaders will undertake the activities listed on the right. We agree. However, the reverse is not true. Coaches do not always act as leaders and that's why we have separate columns. So, our approach to coaching is not 'pure coaching' or 'traditional coaching'.

In pure coaching, you seek only to support others and help them build their solutions through using only their knowledge, words and language. As a traditional coach, you work hard to dismiss your own knowledge outside the coaching process to prevent any bias from affecting the outcome. While we can see this approach may have a place, it both misses an opportunity and ignores the fact that realistically when coaching we are always guiding the process in some way simply because we are asking the questions. Our choice of question always affects what happens next.

What's the difference between coaching and mentoring?

This question is often asked. To start with, the words coaching and mentoring do not always translate well into other languages. It is our understanding from the work we have done that separate words for these constructs do not exist in some languages and there is only one comparable term. Hence, when speaking those languages the English words are used.

The generally accepted essence of a mentor is an individual who has prior experience of the situation the mentee is in, or something similar, and can offer individual advice based on that experience. A mentor advises based on their career and the insights their experience gives them. As an example, a mentor might say: 'When my company moved to a client relationship management process, we found we spent at least six months on data clean-up.'

In this situation, the mentor has specific experience that is relevant and useful to the mentee. Again though, there is not 100% agreement on these terms and you will regularly find consultants who market themselves as coaches and yet regularly move between coaching and mentoring functions. We would argue that this is okay, provided they are explicit about what they do.

Leading or coaching – what mode are you in?

As a leader in coaching mode, your focus will be less on giving advice and more on giving support so that the coachee can think through their own solutions. This does not mean that you let them try anything. You have responsibilities to the business, and also ethically, so you would intervene if your experience or knowledge means you know that a proposed solution is inappropriate.

To give a simple example, you may help a colleague who is feeling stuck on a project to identify possible options to move forward. One of these might be to ask the CEO for advice, and in some businesses and with some CEOs that might be a great idea. In others, such an approach might be career suicide. Or just a waste of time as the CEO would not make time for this. Hence it may be appropriate to 'take off your coaching hat' and offer advice from your experience.

The point we are emphasising is that you need to be clear about your intentions and which role you are playing in each and every conversation. Be clear when you are leading and when you have moved to coaching mode and when you are mentoring too. You cannot be a coach 100% of the time, as sometimes you will need to change gears and mentor, and change gears again and be a boss.

If you find yourself saying 'I need you to do . . . .', you are clearly exercising power and authority and that is not coaching. If, on the other hand, you say 'I like that idea' you may be mentoring someone or, you may be being a boss or you may be coaching. It depends on your intention. All of this emphasises why you must clarify and explain your intentions both for yourself and for the person you are coaching (see Chapter 1).

If you are a leader and also the boss, then trying to coach while still in boss mode means the power dynamic is unclear. Think of power as a baton in a relay race: when you are coaching you pass the baton to your coachee. The spotlight of attention is firmly on them, they are in charge of their learning and their actions, which means that in coaching this is not about *your* needs but about *theirs*. This is a subtle shift, but needs attention or else people will become confused. Learning how to make this shift is one of the main features that you will learn as you work through this book.

Pragmatically, if you coach a member of your team, you will always be their boss. Therefore you always have power which may be unseen and unacknowledged, but it never goes away. However, coaching passes the power of learning to the other person. That is their power, not yours and that's what makes it so exciting. You can never learn for another person – they have to learn for themselves.

Which brings us to another point. Coaching someone is exciting because you see them, before your very eyes, generate new insight into how they operate in the world. So, it is easy to think that coaching is an unalloyed good thing, that it is always the best way to work with someone.

Mostly, we think that this is true. People finding their own answers and their own way forward is the most powerful way to learn. Notwithstanding this point of view, sometimes people simply come up with dippy ideas and when they do, you have three choices.

Your first choice is to be OK with what they come up with – and this is usually the best way to progress because they have the motivation to learn and develop and sometimes that does include making mistakes. So, you have some work to do possibly in letting people have the freedom to experiment and fail.

The second choice is to continue coaching and help them see they're being a bit daft. But this second option comes with a health warning, because now you have a coaching agenda which they may sense and may come to resent. We call this situation 'phoney-coaching' and there's more on it in Part 3: The Pilot's manual.

So, that leaves the third option. You change modes and signal very clearly that you have done so. And then you provide advice or input or direction as their boss. However, this needs to be a clear but nuanced change in focus because some people may feel that you revert too quickly to boss mode and this can damage the relationship for future coaching opportunities.

In short and in pure terms, in coaching the coachee develops and owns the outcomes that best make sense to them. That means as a leader who is in coaching mode, you may need to acknowledge to yourself before you start any conversation that they may end up generating ideas that you don't agree with, or you don't see as sensible. It may be helpful each time you coach to do a quick self-appraisal: Am I genuinely here to help this person grow and develop, including accepting a range of options in this conversation? Simply, if the answer is yes you're cleared for coaching. If the answer is no, you are not embarking on a coaching conversation but a more conventional shaping conversation with you clearly in the role of boss, peer or team member.

What are the key features of coaching?

Here are three key features.

> ### Coachees own the outcomes
>
> Coaching produces insights for your coachee and it is for them to own and act on what they discover. This is a really important understanding to carry with you through this book because many

▶

leaders like to be fixers. After all, that's what most of us have been promoted and praised for in the past – finding what's wrong and putting it right. If you have learned to be a fixer, as you change mode and begin to coach, leave this behind. Now you're acting as a catalyst to someone else taking on the fixing role.

One of the best leaders we know who uses coaching says he feels lazy every time he asks someone else to think it through, but actually he's learnt over the years the more they do the work, the faster the transformation.

You guide the process

When you step into coaching, one of the things you do is guide the process. You make sure that you're not so engaged in the topic that you lose awareness of the trajectory of the conversation, the time allocation and the different tributaries that need exploring.

The skill that is involved in owning the process is called 'meta-cognitive awareness'. We liken this to being in a helicopter where you can look down and see the patterns of conversation and you can see what is happening and what is not happening. This skill of being in a discussion and at the same time being aware of the flux and flow of the discussion is key if you are to shape the discussion.

You can practise this skill every day in every interaction you have, whether it is a specific coaching conversation or popping to the shops to buy your lunch. Taking your awareness up a level will help you become a better coach, and ensures you know how to guide the process.

You focus on the future

Unlike some conversations you might choose to have where it is important to consider 'why', in coaching the emphasis moves to 'what' and 'how'. This very firmly keeps the focus on the future.

> In our experience, a common mistake that leaders make when they coach is to become embroiled in conversations about why something has come about. Understanding the conditions that created a situation may be important for other reasons, such as health and safety or budgeting, but it is often an unhelpful part of coaching because it drags you back into history.
>
> Keep your eyes on the future and you will find coaching can be shorter and more impactful and, quite frankly, more fun.

Coaching skills and behavioural experiments

Throughout this book we're going to coach you to coach and we're going to use a particular device called 'behavioural experiments'. It's a core component of coaching as an enabler of personal change. The basis of behavioural experiments is simple:

- Choose to do one thing differently and consistently over a period of several days or weeks.

- Dispassionately assess what happened as a result of your new approach.

- Include your new, effective behaviour into your personal repertoire.

- Repeat.

- Consider what behaviour you tried that didn't work and modify your approach.

Although we've called them behavioural experiments because they can most obviously be applied to behaviours, the principle of experimentation can also apply to thinking too.

Behavioural experiments lie at the heart of the sections called *Flying Straight and Level* and *Looping the Loop*. In each of these sections, we provide you with a range of ideas to experiment with for yourself. The intention is that they are fun and engaging. It is often helpful to try something more than once before deciding if it works for you and we are strong advocates of this. It is especially true when your instinct or preferences are not to take such a new approach. Practise and reflect on your successes and failures. Consider the differences that you achieved. Keep what works for you and discard what doesn't.

One further point

Many of the interventions we demonstrate and recommend that you experiment with are shorter and more to the point than you might use normally. Of course, we want you to modify our ideas with your culturally appropriate style but please be sure to understand the principle behind our suggestions.

The chapters in this book are deliberately short. In under ten minutes you've understood the issues and are ready to practise. They are aimed at shaping behaviour and thinking (small nudges in the right direction, not 180 degrees of change). There is an ongoing emphasis on how to do, think and play with new ideas, search for new solutions – and be better.

The safety briefing

We will steal shamelessly from our flying analogy to draw your attention to some items of safety. It's important, if not critical, you know about some situations that might arise in coaching and some safe ways to handle them.

SITUATION 1: STRESS, ANXIETY OR DEPRESSION

Imagine that someone you are coaching mentions to you that they are highly stressed, anxious or depressed. While the new-norm might be for everyone to claim they are stressed and wear it as a badge of honour, there are people who are vulnerable and do need help. Stress can become over-whelming, it can be associated with burnout and it can compromise mental wellness. If you clearly hear that someone is not coping this is a cry for help and you need to know how to transition smoothly to another type of conversation. As a leader of people with or without direct reports, it is your responsibility to look out for these situations. Missing them can be catastrophic for the individual and the organisation.

When you hear such a cry for help, this is no longer simply a coaching conversation. This is about how they get the mental and emotional support they need to return to wellness. We advocate focusing your attention on listening to understand and empathise (see Chapter 8 on empathy) with a view to agreeing when next you might talk (see Chapter 10 on action setting). The primary purpose of creating this time before speaking again – which may be later the same day and should certainly be very soon – is to enable you to remind yourself of the procedures and support available.

If you work for a large firm, you will probably have access to an employee assistance programme (EAP). As a leader and one who coaches, you need to know what services are available via the EAP and how to refer people to the programme. If you don't have an EAP provider, be sure to contact human resources to get their help and support. At all times you will need to recognise the need for appropriate levels of confidentiality.

SITUATION 2: DIFFICULT DISCLOSURE

Imagine someone you are coaching tells you something, in confidence, that is illegal, a conflict of interest or potentially harmful. Between us, we have heard stories of domestic violence, corporate sabotage and border-line suicide statements. Although you would normally expect to keep the content of a coaching conversation confidential, there are instances when you just can't. These are some of them.

Equally, subject to the laws of the land in which you work, you can't just unilaterally raise the alarm and break your coachee's confidence. If you are faced with this sort of situation, you need to be clear with your coachee that what you have just heard is sufficiently alarming for you to want to involve another professional. Then have a discussion with them about what they've said and how jointly you will approach the appropriate authorities or services.

Jenny, having faced these situations several times in her coaching career, now carries with her the phone numbers for the Samaritans and MIND, both of which are charities with excellent helplines that anyone can use. Although these organisations might be unavailable in your country, there may be equivalents that you can research and have ready if needed.

Resources

One more addition you'd expect. It's a bit of extra hand luggage that will fit neatly into the overhead locker. Suggestions for further reading, listening (podcasts) or watching (videos/YouTube) are provided for each area we address.

Your flight plan for take-off

Whether you reviewed this *Welcome on board* at speed or took your time, you may find it helpful to quickly answer the following questions to embed the key lessons in this section:

- What is one action you might take in leading mode?

- What is one action you might take in coaching mode?

- What is one hallmark of coaching?

- Who owns the outcomes of coaching?

- Who guides the process of coaching?

- What self-appraisal might you do before starting to coach?

Seatbelts on? Enjoy your flight . . .

Navigation – help with classic leadership challenges

The purpose of this book is for leaders to identify critical skills and develop them to increase their overall leadership and management strengths. We do this by focussing on the skill of coaching and its component parts. And yet, while you are developing your capabilities on a daily basis, you are likely to be faced with immediate leadership issues. Ones where you do not have the time to read the whole book, practise all the skills and then apply them wholesale. You have to address the problem today. And you may feel uncertain as to which particular skill or skills you need in order to address the issue. So what do you do? You use this chapter.

When you need a Fast Track to a solution to a specific issue the tables we provide below set out tools and techniques to move you forward today. We can do this because in our coaching experience we notice that many leadership challenges crop up again and again. Equally, when we talk with coachees and leaders about these challenges they can easily provide their own answers. And these answers tend to be very similar too.

Leaders and managers the world over use similar techniques to successfully address similar issues. And what's missing is very rarely *knowledge*. The focus of most coaching is on personal behaviour change and the mental or emotional blockers that get in the way of individual change. Here we use our experience to offer a place to start, using a coaching approach, to help you progress quickly on many of these issues.

Of course, people are all individuals and they will do things differently. We are not arguing that the same tool or technique is always appropriate. Nor are we arguing that tools should be used in a specific order in a given situation. Rather, we are saying that in these given situations certain tools and techniques regularly appear to be beneficial. Hence, when you do not have time to learn everything first, and when you are wondering which techniques may be helpful, we offer a place to start.

And so at this point, we need to issue a huge caveat. Making behaviour change simple (which is our aim in this book) is not becoming simplistic (which we're actively avoiding). Sometimes change is easy. But humans are complex creatures, so please don't think that because we have tried to lay things out in a clear and uncomplicated way that we are diminishing how difficult it can be sometimes.

We list in the tables some of the most typical situations that leaders face and alongside each challenge we provide one or two jewels from the coaching toolkit that might help to unlock or shift the situation. Other tools will be helpful too. In offering this simple approach, we lay ourselves open to criticism that we've been simplistic. So please believe us when we say we know it can be messy, non-linear and difficult, but we are also convinced that these tables are a feature that makes this book unique.

Ideally, you will use the nuggets that we suggest alongside many of the other tools that are available. That said, if you are really stuck, here are our ideas of how to get unstuck. And, of course, if this still leaves you uncertain, feel free to contact us at www.coachingonthego.co.uk.

You are the best judge of your situation and the people you work with. Adjust our suggestions to make them appropriate to your culture and your company.

Use this look-up table to Fast Track to new coaching solutions.

We hope you enjoy stretching your wings.

Fast Track look-up tables

Challenges with individuals who report to you

What you see happening	Our Fast Track solution	Page
New behaviour you want to encourage.	Catch the right thing and give praise in a timely manner.	49
Work is sub-optimal – consistently late, not good enough or passed inappropriately to someone else for action.	Use STARTER™ or SBI to give feedback that is straight-forward and timely.	43, 182
Not working at the strategic level that they can or should – overly involved in detail.	Use delegation techniques to enable them to see what level you need them to operate at.	118
Dumping work up or down – too much gets escalated or too much gets passed down to others.	Help them to recognise what they are doing through creating awareness.	82
Consistent complaints of a lack of time.	Use the Up Down and Around model to uncover where they think they spend their time and use generative listening to uncover hidden assumptions.	95, 106
Lack of motivation and commitment.	Use the sentence stem 'I notice . . . ' to begin the conversation.	89
Consistent underperformance and you need to figure out the root cause.	Use naming to get started then use Pause-Points™ to stay present and help them to speak.	89, 62
Overwhelmed by workload, stressed and not prioritising well.	Use powerful questions to uncover their point of view.	178

What you see happening	Our Fast Track solution	Page
Thinking they are ready to be a team leader but they are not.	Use the technique of different perspectives to help them understand the different opinions.	94
Denying or ignoring commercial pressures.	Create a SMART action plan.	130
Not creative in finding solutions and overly rigid, requiring more innovation and flexibility.	Share the situational leadership model with them to provide a framework on how you are trying to work with them.	155
Despite coaching and prompting, rarely identifying areas of improvement for themselves.	Explore the Johari Window and the activities we offer to help them gain confidence in sharing more of themselves. Be prepared to acknowledge that this person may not be willing to be coached – and consider how that affects their long-term role in your team.	159
Unwilling to share ideas with colleagues, withholding valuable knowledge from the team.	Use the when/then statement structure to demonstrate the consequences of this behaviour. Design a reflection intervention so they begin to notice their underlying assumptions.	89–90, 140
A difficult situation, such as bullying.	Give honest, straightforward feedback using the STARTER™ and SBI models. Use the tools around uncovering hidden assumptions to drill down to understand what is happening.	43, 182, 159
Severe depression or anxiety.	Before starting the conversation have resources to hand to signpost them to. Take advice from others, such as human resources or your employee assistance programme to understand how to hand over to them if needed. Use phrases based on 'I notice . . . .' to neutrally describe what you observe. If the conversation does uncover a mental or emotional wellness issue, hand over to other professionals and encourage the individual to see their doctor.	18

Challenges with the team who report to you

What you see happening	Our Fast Track solution	Page
Conflict between team members.	Use generative listening and Pause-Points™ to get underneath the symptoms and find the root cause. Use the paired listening technique to build willingness to hear each other's perspectives.	106, 62, 114
Tight-knit team with a new joiner coming into a new key role.	Role-playing the different perspectives exercise, using the new joiner as one of the perspectives. Create a SMART action plan with the group.	95, 129
Conflict between team members.	Use naming to get them to identify the issue and then use their naming as the foundation of the conversation. Use reflection techniques to enable colleagues to share their thoughts and feelings while being respected.	140, 89
Struggling to adjust to organisational change.	Consider whether to talk to individuals first or whether this is something to work on as a group. Use the drama triangle as a way of exploring their attitude to the changes.	173

Challenges with your boss or a peer

What you see happening	Our Fast Track solution	Page
Making requests thoughtlessly of others – prone to asking in emails for large reports or data sets or significant investigations without thinking through the work involved.	Use when/then statements to frame the issue. Invite them to do a different perspectives exercise.	94, 89–90
Setting goals that you feel unable to influence.	Use naming to get them to identify the issue and then use their naming as the foundation of the conversation.	89

▶

25

What you see happening	Our Fast Track solution	Page
Goes to your direct reports to give tasks that you have previously agreed are not a priority.	Use the situational leadership model to explain how you are trying to work for them and hence illustrating where their actions reduce your learning and effectiveness.	155
Your boss keeps moving the goal posts so you struggle to deliver effectively.	Use contracting each time you discuss actions including an aim to agree the next steps. Use when/then statements to confirm back your understanding when talking. Use SMART goals to send your understanding in writing after each meeting.	30, 94, 130
When conflict arises between departments, yours always seems to suffer.	Invite your peers to do a different perspective exercise – especially before a negotiation commences. Ask your peer(s) to sit in your shoes, and where there are more than two parties everyone shifts perspective and represents the other's department.	96
Your boss does not seem to listen to you or to respect your opinion.	Gain permission to challenge your boss. Introduce your boss to the STARTER™ and SBI models explaining how you are using them with your peers and team members. In due course, use these techniques with your boss.	33, 43, 182
You are not clear what your boss wants from you.	Ask your boss questions using the Up, Down and Around™ model to identify the implications of your actions on others around you.	95

Part 2

The main flight

Main Flight

COACHING
ON THE GO

COACHING ON THE GO
JULY 3

AIR MAIL

How to lead your team
effectively in 10 minutes a day

Chapter 1

First things first: chocks away!

Caroline
CO-PILOT

Where to start the conversation

How many times have you been to a meeting only to find yourself annoyed by the lack of clarity on what you are there to achieve, how you are going to achieve it and total uncertainty on what's happening next? Our guess is that most of us think we have too many meetings like that. Surprisingly in some ways, this problem is closely linked to a fundamental part of coaching known as contracting. This is where your coaching conversation starts – and we strongly recommend applying this logic to all business conversations.

When we use the word contracting, we don't mean a piece of paper but an understanding that lies between you and the coachee. The underlying principle is to check in with your employee, colleague or team so you have a consistent understanding of the practical and contextual issues surrounding the conversation. Simple issues such as how long might the conversation be and its purpose. For example, is the coachee seeking advice or looking for coaching?

In coaching, effective contracting has the impact of building trust and psychological safety. As covered in Welcome on board in Part 1 this is especially important when you are the boss or there is some form of power relationship between you. The coachee needs to believe they can openly share their thinking without fear of your judgement, given the professional development nature of such coaching. This act of contracting helps all parties to understand where they stand and how it differs from the usual day-to-day relationship.

Making this change of focus noticeable is fundamental to contracting. The most important and first principle of coaching is that the content of a coaching conversation is confidential and will remain strictly between the parties involved. This is not as clear-cut as it might sound. Furthermore, in business coaching, where the content of the discussion is likely to be a business issue, there is an added complexity as to where to draw the line.

We suggest you think of confidentiality as always applying to the specifics of the learning component and how the coachee is developing, rather than the operational tasks or business issues underlying them. The important point of confidentiality in contracting is that you consider such issues actively and address them openly in order to create a safe space for the coachee to explore their own thinking. This includes being able to put aside animosities or other issues that might get in the way.

Professional coaches often use a model called the Three Ps of Contracting. You may find it helpful as it guides you to recall the issues you may want to address at the start of any conversation – not just when you plan to use your coaching skills.

Procedure:

- How long do we have for this conversation? When will we talk next?

- Are we in a suitable location (to avoid being overheard or interrupted)?

- Can we turn our phones off to improve our concentration?

- What do you/we want to achieve from this discussion?

- Can you make notes of what you decide to do next?

Professional:

- Is this a confidential chat?

- Is this a coaching conversation? Or am I directing you as your line manager?

- What are we here for and how can I help?

Psychological:

- How open to challenge are you today?

- How supportive do you want me to be?

- What might get in the way of my efforts to help you?

- What boundaries are there to our chat, e.g. not talking about personal issues?

Coaching *On-the-Go* doesn't require us to check every point in these three Ps, but it is a helpful structure to think through before you jump into the subject matter.

Why do we contract?

Outlining boundaries and clarifying expectations allows everyone to know what to expect. A quick compact conversation about each other's expectations is often a great step to building trust and openness. It can also have a calming effect which is valuable in many stressful business situations.

When we teach the principles of contracting we ask people to practise it. Initially on its own and then every time they practise an element of the coaching skillset. This feels very unnatural at first for many people and you may feel you are stating the obvious. Perhaps with respect to simple process issues such as how long is the meeting for. And yet, who among us has not been asked for two minutes of our time only to be still talking 20 minutes later? And who has been reaching the peak of their sales message only for the client to announce that the meeting may be in their diary for an hour but they have to leave in five minutes?

Leaders consistently feed back to us the value of contracting. This is because the positive impact of a well-understood contract goes beyond that of coaching. In any conversation or meeting people feel much more confident about the conversation when there is clear contracting at its start. People are able to stand up and say, 'Hang on. I'm not sure I actually need to be part of this conversation. Am I okay to leave?' Or they might say, 'Actually, I don't need any help with the outsourcing project. Where I'm really stuck is following next year's budgeting rules.'

We have worked with an organisation over a couple of years helping to create a coaching culture across the business. Contracting is consistently one of the most positive impacts described in the feedback due to the increase in effectiveness it generates.

Effective contracting can be especially useful when working relationships seem to be deteriorating, where parties seem to be forming assumptions about others' perspectives and where meetings seem to become less friendly over time. This arises because people can agree on these simple things quickly and this puts more of a positive frame on the discussions moving forward. It can also help sort out the basic questions: What do we think we are here to do? What's our goal?

Gaining permission

One of the positive impacts of clear contracting is the agreement on the different roles each person is playing (coach, mentor, coachee) and the focus of the conversation. This gives the parties permission to talk about the subject without treading on anyone's toes. This process of seeking permission has a much broader impact which runs throughout coaching.

Often, we are faced with very challenging business issues, where people feel they have a vested interest or a position they should defend. This affects how they listen and how they respond in discussions. Acknowledging the significance of the issue and seeking explicit permission to move the conversation into the more difficult areas can help to lower these defences and make people more open to challenge.

At its simplest this could be, 'Do you mind if I challenge you on that point?' It is rare for a coachee to say that they mind being challenged, although such a response would be powerful and important for you to hear. The more likely response is a positive one and a readiness to a challenge that they have, in principle, accepted.

If you are not used to this idea it can feel strange and slightly forced at first. And yet coachees do notice a change in themselves by being made ready for a challenge. Jenny's preferred approach is: 'I need to challenge something. Can we stop and just explore this for a moment?' It is asking permission to explore, which makes the challenge much easier to hear. Presented in a reasonable manner, the position is accepted.

It would rarely make sense to reject such a request, although there could be the exception when someone is feeling stressed and *yet another* challenge would be too much right then. And you need to be attuned to this possibility. It does not happen often and yet the reply could be an honest, 'Actually I am feeling really stressed at the moment and I'm not sure I could take any more.' In this case you should provide the appropriate support and look for another more suitable opportunity (see the Safety Briefing in Part 1).

This act of seeking permission can work very well when managing upwards, when working with someone senior to you. For example, 'I'm beginning to think I was looking at this in a different way to you, so do you mind if

I share my thinking?' Or simply, 'Could I play devil's advocate for a moment just to test the ground?' In accepting this request your boss has given you permission to challenge their thinking or their world view. Of course, this is not permission to tell them they're an idiot, so you need to be tactful. Without forgetting that you have been allowed to demonstrate that they might be wrong or that an alternative approach has greater merit.

Time to fly. . .

Sometimes it is hard to imagine how new phrases or new behaviour might look or feel. Often adopting new approaches can be helped by seeing how someone else does it. We now start our story which illustrates the tools, techniques and skills in a true-to-life scenario. In the story we follow the trials and tribulations of a team working at the global, fictitious airline UsFlyHiPo. You may like to look back at the Cast List in Part 1.

After each scene of the story we offer *Flying Straight and Level* options (the easier choice) and *Looping the Loop* options (a more advanced choice). This is the critical point where you are invited to practise the coaching skills yourself. If you fancy a challenge, or feel this is a skill you are already quite good at, go straight to *Looping the Loop*. If you prefer to take a steadier route, start first with *Flying Straight and Level*.

If one experiment doesn't work, have a go with something different. New habits take time to get established so don't rush yourself and keep an open mind as to how you can adapt these ideas to suit your specific situation. When your experiment does not go as planned, avoid rushing to the conclusion that it doesn't work. Instead, take time to do a small modification and try again. We recommend you read through the *Flying Straight and Level* options even if you plan to move straight to the harder options as they may stimulate a useful activity nonetheless.

And now to the story where our narrator, the air traffic controller, starts us off.

Meet Caroline the Co-Pilot at UsFlyHiPo. She is literally a high-flyer. She has the potential for further greatness. She normally flies large passenger jets with her senior companion, Prya the Pilot.

Their journey begins as Caroline is about to meet with FC, her line manager, to hear the results of an assessment panel which she needs to pass to be awarded a promotion. Before facing him, Caroline has sought out Tomacz, one of the crew members, for a chat in the canteen. But her motives are suspect and Tomacz will have none of it.

SCENE 1: CAROLINE THE CO-PILOT PREPARES

'So tell me,' Caroline asks Tomacz, 'who do you think was to blame in Istanbul?'

Tomacz moves casually to the side forcing Caroline slightly away from the other people around them: 'Hmm, that's an interesting way to phrase the question. What leads you to ask? What is it you want to hear?'

'Oh,' says Caroline avoiding eye contact. 'I'm just interested.'

Tomacz pauses and asks, 'So is this a confidential conversation then? What do you mean when you say you are just interested?'

'Yes, of course it's confidential. I'd like to know what other people think.'

'Well,' Tomacz cautions, 'How will that help you?'

'It just will.' Caroline is emphatic and feels slightly annoyed.

'I need to challenge you. Is that okay?' asks Tomacz.

'Of course.' Caroline nods with a knot tightening in her stomach.

'What makes it so important to you?'

Caroline reflects and answers, 'I'm not sure'. Tomacz patiently waits while she thinks some more. 'Maybe I'm worried people are blaming me for it.'

'Ah, thanks for sharing that with me. You're worried people are blaming you for it. How useful is that to you?'

Gosh, thought Caroline. What a weird question. A bit daft really. You know, if she thought about it, and reflected a bit, she knew she wanted to know, but she couldn't really think of how it would be useful to her at all. But surely it would be valuable in some way and why was Tomacz being so unhelpful?

'Well surely I have a right to know. I'm having my annual review with FC this afternoon. I need to make sure the facts are generally known. People just make stuff up. How can I trust them if I don't know what they think?'

'Frankly,' Tomacz was blunt, 'If that's the way you're thinking, you've got lots more important things to worry about. You need to understand how this place works, see the wood for the trees. FC is one of the best leaders I've met and believe me, I've worked with a few. Your review is part of the development process and you need to focus on that.' He smiled at her to take any sting out of his comments. 'C'mon, you've got to learn!' He paused to size up her reaction. 'Look. I'm really happy to help you. When you are ready to focus on the right stuff, feel free to come back to me.'

And with that he walked away.

Caroline could not have been more irritated.

Your turn at the controls

What actions did you notice Tomacz take which illustrated the skill of contracting in an unplanned conversation? Take a moment to look back and identify these.

Consider how he:

- ensures the conversation cannot be overheard by physically moving away from others

- checks with Caroline by asking 'Is this a confidential conversation?'

- avoids rushing to simply answer the question, but instead pauses to check her motivations with, 'What is it that you want to hear?'

Now let's give you a variety of exercises to practice this contracting technique yourself.

 FLYING STRAIGHT AND LEVEL

1. Set a goal for the following week to practise contracting and put ten minutes into your diary afterwards to reflect on what you learned.

In every business conversation and meeting you are involved in, whether you are leading it or participating, whenever you can, start with some basic contracting questions (assuming no one else deals with it first). Use these examples or a variation on them:

- Can I just check how long this meeting (or conversation) will last? How long have we got?

- Can we agree to turn off our phones or does anyone need to leave theirs on for emergency purposes?

- May I check, what input do you want from me in this conversation?

- What's the outcome we are aiming to achieve from this?

Make a note at the end of each day as to how often you did this, how this compares to normal and how useful it felt. A separate notebook for this purpose (paper or phone) can be very helpful. You can use it to capture how the exercises work for you throughout this book. In the time you set aside to reflect, look back through these and ask yourself:

- What worked well for me?

- When did it have most impact?

- How can I use this to improve next week?

▶

2. After that first week, try a further experiment aimed at revealing the real intentions of a conversation and getting clarity on what's actually at stake. Put ten minutes aside in your diary at the end of the next three days and reflect on the conversations you have had with people that day and ask yourself:

- How did people frame conversations they had with you? Did they give you enough clarity to help them effectively?

- What was obscure, unexpressed or under-explored?

- What sorts of additional information might have helped our conversation?

- What is the best question you could have asked to get the conversation broader or deeper?

- What were your assumptions? What do you think were their assumptions?

Repeat this practice until you feel comfortable that you understand the issues of contracting and it has started to become your autopilot setting.

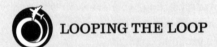 **LOOPING THE LOOP**

When you are ready, have a go at these more advanced approaches. If you chose to start by *Flying Straight and Level*, you may have begun to notice that in real time you develop a sense of where to add a pause and a question.

1. People often frame a conversation obscurely. Take time to clarify their real intention or request and see what difference it makes. For example, you can practise when colleagues are seeking your help. Try asking:

- That's interesting, what's behind that request/statement?

- What sort of help or feedback from me would be most useful at this point?

- Tell me a bit more, would you?

- Let's clarify our roles in this conversation: what perspective should we be taking?

Take time to notice what happens in your conversations and your relationships. At the end of the day, take ten minutes to reflect on these conversations and notice what is happening given this new approach.

This practice invites you to try the following in real time:

- When you are about to dive in and share your opinion: first, stop and pause.
- Find your best question **not** your best answer (at least not yet).

Repeat this practice until you feel comfortable that you understand the issues of confidentiality and contracting.

2. Finally, just a note that you can use this concept in an email-heavy culture too. We've found that in more and more industries emails flood in with work requests or instructions. Pick up the phone and ask some simple contracting questions:

- What specifically do you need?
- What's your minimum requirement?
- What else is affected by what I deliver?

These are great clarifying questions which can prevent a lot of extra wasted work – and they are much more effective than sending an email back hoping the next response will provide that clarity.

THINGS TO DO BEFORE THE NEXT FLIGHT

Read Peter Block's '*Flawless Consulting: A Guide to Getting your Expertise Used*', published in 2011 by John Wiley & Sons.

If you want a funny video on the principle of coaching to understand that our job as a coach is not to fix, watch 'It's Not About The Nail' visit our website www.coachingonthego.co.uk where we provide the latest link.

Listen to our podcast series, sponsored by Cranfield University where several leaders talk about how they have coached people to help them see how they can achieve their potential. You'll find the latest link to these on our website www.coachingonthego.co.uk.

For further resources go to: www.coachingonthego.co.uk

Chapter 2

Giving feedback: revving up

GLOBAL HEAD OF FLYING STAFF

Use STARTER™ to encourage and shape behaviour

At some point in our working lives most of us move from being in a team to leading a team. You may be the boss in the hierarchical sense and hold positional power – you have been promoted. Alternatively, you may be asked to run a project or have just stepped up to lead an activity. This too makes you a boss.

When you become a boss your ability to give feedback will affect the overall outcomes. The skill of feedback also plays an important part in coaching because the coach is there to help the coachee notice what they are saying and thinking. And to bring to the coachee's attention any implicit assumptions or beliefs which are affecting what they do – negatively or positively.

The very word 'feedback' might cause you to shudder. In some cultures, the word is sadly entirely consistent with negativity. When someone says they want to give you some feedback your first thought might be 'Oh gosh. What have I done wrong (now)?' This type of reaction is a very good reason to find ways to share feedback in a way that people don't have that reaction, but can instead, learn.

'Feedback is the breakfast of champions'.

Ken Blanchard

Ken Blanchard is a world-renowned management expert. Why did he (allegedly) first say this about feedback? Blanchard was drawing attention to the fact that feedback is an ongoing and consistent practice required to generate great performance. So that applies to you too (go and get some feedback) as well as to those around you so that you can motivate them towards greater performance.

Feedback is not a one-off exercise, given when something has gone wrong, rather it is a regular process. It helps people to develop, learn and improve in ways that matter to them. Feedback also has to help people see what you expect as you're the boss, or help them see what is expected by the project leader they're seconded to, or other stakeholders too.

In our terms, feedback is the process of providing a coachee with information on what you think would be beneficial for them to hear that might improve their ability to contribute. It may be doing more of the same thing in the same way, or, it might be changing a way of doing something. Crucially it needs to make sense to them and they need to be able to internalise this information. And you want to reach the point where giving and receiving feedback is a habit – when it is a habit, you will find yourself asking for it regularly.

You cannot predict how your feedback will be received. However well you think you know the coachee, you do not know their state of mind when you approach them. Contracting is a crucial way to reduce the uncertainty, especially with tough feedback. For example, you might say, 'Is this a good time for us to speak?' or 'Let's just step away from our current work as I have something important and potentially challenging to talk to you about.'

Here is our easy formula for giving feedback: STARTER™.

1. **S** = Start well and contract	Don't spend too long on pleasantries. Have a small chat to help set a constructive mood. Use your contracting skills (see Chapter 1) by saying for example, 'Part of my role is coaching you and to help you be your best. We just need ten minutes.'
2. **T** = Topic at the heart of the feedback	Set out what you're there to talk about – note, not your evaluation – just the subject, for example: 'I want to review how you got on with xyz' or 'I want to review your presentation to the ABC project team.' Be very specific to allow you both to evaluate and understand the situation. Generalities create confusion and disagreement.
3. **A** = Ask for their self-assessment	Listen to their views, by asking some (not all) of the following: • How are you getting on? • What are the challenges you're facing? • What are you really enjoying? • What are you struggling with? • What are our key stakeholders feeling right now? • What would others say? • What are you really pleased about? • Who's helping you? • What's surprised you? • How strategic are you being?

	The purpose of asking such questions is to enable the coachee to find their own feedback. Remember the coaching principles, from Part 1 and get them to do the work. In a perfect world they will identify the same need for change as you have. And together you can agree a new way forward.
	To be effective with this step when giving challenging feedback, you need to consider your overall relationship with the coachee. Asking questions in this way is taking a coaching approach and yet there is a risk of *phoney-coaching* (more on this later in Part 3: The Pilot's manual).
4. **R** = Revise or Reinforce from another perspective	If step 3 has not resulted in a good way forward or has not fully addressed what you need your coachee to understand, your job is then to modify their self-assessment. Do so by offering a different perspective which you must own and agree with. Otherwise it will not be authentic.
	'Yes, I've heard that too' is reinforcing. 'That's not how I see it' offers a contrary perspective. 'I like your assessment of ABC, but think you might consider XYZ too' provides a broader perspective, while 'The feedback from stakeholder 123 is that . . . ' gives a straightforward appraisal. Be very specific about the actions that were taken and the consequences they had so that you can be equally clear on what you would like done differently.
	Our experience is that if you do steps 1 to 3 above well, then this step is a doddle. Most people are naturally self-critical, self-aware or self-correcting if we just give them space to notice and express it. When they don't come forward with an honest appraisal it is usually because they don't yet truly believe that you're there to help them. That is a different story, but an important one, and if this is your frequent experience, then we suggest this says something about your leadership.

5. **T** = Test what they heard and understood	Use your contracting skills again, for example: 'To avoid any uncertainty, tell me what you think we've agreed will happen next?' 'What parts of this are you less sure about?' or 'What do you think?'
	The answers may require you to repeat step 4.
6. **E** = Exploration time, so they can soak it in	Acknowledge that the coachee might want time to soak the message in, but don't brush it under the carpet. Examples might be:
	'This is important for us to respond to, so could you soak on what you've heard over night and we can pick this up in the morning.'
	'I don't want us to treat this lightly, how about you get back to me with some next steps by the end of tomorrow.'
	'This feedback at this point is a real gift because it gives us the possibility to 'course-correct' early. Sleep on it and come see me tomorrow.'
7. **R** = Review and agree next steps	Set aside another time to follow up and make sure you do.

There are a few reasons why giving feedback may not be effective and you need to consider these as you start to practise your technique so that you can adjust your style:

- The coachee feels wronged or exasperated by the content of what they heard: 'That's just not true.'

- The coachee feels outraged that someone without credibility has dared to challenge them: 'How the hell do **they** know?'

- The coachee feels their sense of identity has been attacked causing a sense of defensiveness and being overwhelmed: 'How dare you?'

Our technique above is designed to reduce the possibility of these issues.

Feedback – both praise and course-correction – is a foundational skill for coaching. Without feedback, people simply don't know how well they are doing. If they're doing well, you want them to know that and you probably want them to do more of the same sort of thing. If they're not doing well, you *need* them to know so you can both begin the process of shaping new behaviour. From a coaching perspective you are helping your coachee notice their reality, enabling their awareness and so helping them on a journey of change. Or if they prefer, and it is acceptable for your business, they can still decide to remain where they are.

Never ever shy away from giving feedback. If you find yourself reluctant to give it, then the section *your turn at the controls* at the end of this chapter offers some ideas to discover why and to start to change your practice. As you consider when to give tough feedback make sure the coachee has time and space to reflect on it without affecting their work – and this does not mean the end of the day or the end of the week.

We strongly recommend against the Friday conversation. It's a classic error. It may feel good as you have taken something difficult off your to-do list and you've time to reflect on it, but you have just ruined their evening or weekend. When you anticipate your coachee may need time to reflect on your feedback you could specifically suggest that they go for a walk or for a coffee before returning back to their desk.

And one final thing. We do not advocate the feedback sandwich. If you have not heard of this, that's good. It is also known in many circles as the 'Sh*t sandwich'. Many people argue that for constructive feedback to be heard it should be sandwiched between two pieces of uniquely positive feedback. Given that we believe feedback should be given in a timely manner and continuously it makes no sense to us to save things up. And we think it is perceived as totally disingenuous as people learn that shortly after some positive feedback they are likely to get developmental feedback and hence they fail to listen.

Given the importance of feedback, here's how it goes in our story (not so well as it happens).

You will recognise the next scene because we've all been there, some of us from both sides of the fence. Caroline is meeting with FC for her annual review at the airline's international swanky HQ.

FC is the global lead of flying staff. Caroline is beginning to feel let down as she waits for FC to finish. The truth is, she's caught up in her own thoughts, ruminating again on the incident in Istanbul. Despite the incident, she knows she could do Prya's job and she's sure she's ready for that promotion.

FC is closing up the conversation.

SCENE 2: CAROLINE MEETS FC

'The feedback I've been getting is definitely positive,' FC says to Caroline. 'I see lots of evidence that you are continuing to grow. Yet, as I have illustrated, you are not ready for the next step up – you haven't sufficiently demonstrated the behaviours we expect of captains.'

Caroline looks crestfallen. Unable to stop herself from arguing, she splutters, 'It's the incident in Istanbul, isn't it? You need a scapegoat and that's me'.

'No that's not correct,' replies FC. 'I'm not evaluating your technical skills. I'm looking carefully at your leadership capability and mindset. We all represent the global brand here at UsFlyHiPo, and you represent a key part of the whole as we all do. To the best of our ability we want passengers to react positively even if their trip has been a nightmare. You are part of a team and you still need to work at demonstrating that you are a team player. I've given you examples that indicate I'm not yet convinced. Don't be misled by the incident in Istanbul. Prya has made it very clear how difficult that was. My decision on your next step is unaffected by that one incident. You need to demonstrate you can . . . '

But Caroline is no longer listening. She is so upset that she doesn't hear how FC is trying to help her with offers of coaching support.

▶

What had Prya said to FC about her? Had Prya shifted blame on to Caroline? 'I know I can do her job and lead the team,' she thought. 'They should just give me the opportunity and I'll prove it. It's all about regulations and restrictions around here. Why should I sit around and wait when I know I can do this? Surely, I'd walk straight into her job at another airline. There's nothing she does that I couldn't do . . . '

FC realises that Caroline is no longer listening. He's disappointed and yet it fits with the earlier feedback and the examples he gave her about her willingness to learn. He will look for another opportunity to help and, as they separate, he asks her to reflect carefully on the conversation.

'What was FC saying?' thought Caroline as she walked away, 'Something about reflections . . . or was it reactions . . . ?'

Your turn at the controls

In our story FC demonstrates that success is not guaranteed. The state of mind of the receiver is always key and, on this occasion, FC knows that Caroline is simply not receptive to the feedback. This is an important skill within the feedback process.

 FLYING STRAIGHT AND LEVEL

1. Reflect on your own reactions and experiences of feedback:
   - Have you ever received feedback that was genuinely helpful to your growth and development? If you have, we're sure you'll agree it was a

gift, allowing you to recalibrate your performance, your contribution and meet the expectations of your boss.

- Have you ever received feedback that made you proud of your achievements? If you have, we're sure you won't have forgotten. Also, we're pretty sure that you relished working for that person or in that project. Feedback can be a great motivator.

- Have you ever had a discussion of your performance that left you hurt, demoralised or angry or damaged your self-esteem? If you have, is it this type of experience that is making you a reluctant provider of feedback? We suggest that you re-frame your expectation of feedback from a difficult and hurtful experience to an enlightening and positive one. You can become skilful in providing your coachees with feedback. Read on to learn how.

2. Actively look for situations to give team members feedback regarding something they have done well and you want them to continue to do. Use the STARTER™ framework and don't just jump to the praise part but work systematically through all the steps. Starting with simple positive feedback is an easier place to build your new habit. By team members we mean someone working for you who therefore can expect guidance and development. If you do not have team members, offer the feedback to juniors or peers. Challenge yourself to identify such situations and offer feedback on these actions at least three times every week from now on.

Using our STARTER™ technique make a note of any consequences in how you feel and how your team members or colleagues react.

Be a little cautious. If you have not been in the habit of doing this in the past, people are likely to notice the change. This means you will need to continue with this behaviour to make it normal.

Try these phrases and make up some of your own:

- I really liked how you did . . .
- Great job on . . .
- Thanks so much for . . .
- You exceeded my expectations on . . .
- Really appreciate all your efforts on . . .

▶

As you start modelling the behaviour of praise, you might notice that others also begin to do this more among the team, so over time it will become second nature to everyone. Occasionally, if this is particularly new behaviour, someone might ask about it, 'What's up? You've never made such a comment in the past.' If this happens, great job – they've noticed a change. We suggest you respond head-on. 'Yeah. I've been reading this book about coaching and leadership skills and I'm following their guidance to practise some of the ideas. What do you think?'

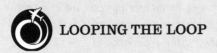

LOOPING THE LOOP

For your masterclass in giving feedback, we're proposing that you first learn how to give smaller doses of feedback more frequently.

1. List four people in your team who could do better. Alongside each name write down the most helpful feedback you could provide each person. Particularly write down things that you think they're blind to, or that is not absolutely clear to them. Examples include: you are a natural leader, you have quiet authority, you have a way of working that stakeholders appreciate. Don't shy away from feedback that is aimed at course-correction, simply think about how you'd like to receive it if you were in their shoes.

   Use this matrix of individual feedback to try out your new coaching skills. Remember, no shortcuts. Start with contracting, then use our feedback formula STARTER™ to give you a structure. As before, keep notes, reflect on what you notice. Keep at it and refine your skills.

   Gradually, as you get more fluent in these skills of contracting and giving feedback, you might find these are almost part of your daily conversations.

2. Now you can start to give yourself an even greater challenge as a coach. Think about your succession pipeline, think about who on your team needs developing as a potential successor. You probably want to have more than one person in mind. Again, start by writing their names down.

Now consider what feedback would be helpful for them to hear so that they can develop skills or have relevant experiences to make them ready to step into your role.

Here are a couple of examples:

- We need to find opportunities for you to have more exposure with the senior leadership team. Your profile would benefit from them seeing more of you. How might you do this?

- I can see that you're still uncomfortable presenting to a senior audience. Let's think about how you can improve at this. Maybe we can give you more experience doing this sort of presentation, with me supporting you?

Eventually, through these types of coaching conversation, you will create more capacity in the team. Each team member will be more effective – an outcome that is good for them and for you too.

3. Finally, let's move to the hardest type of feedback for many, where something needs to change as the existing approach is having a negative effect on the individual or organisation's performance.

By now you may be practised at giving positive feedback. This will help. Of course, you may not have that luxury if something has happened today that needs corrective action.

Actively look out for such situations. It may be something you have been putting off for a while. Prepare yourself using our STARTER™ technique. Take a moment to practise what you want to say – in your head or in brief written notes or even out loud. Look for the most appropriate situation if you can take time to do so, for example, when you think morale will be good. And go for it.

Keep practising.

THINGS TO DO BEFORE THE NEXT FLIGHT

Read Ken Blanchard and Spencer Johnson's *'The New One Minute Manager'* published in 2015 by Manjul Publishing.

We follow Dr Marshall Goldsmith on LinkedIn for general advice on coaching: if you check him out, you might want to follow him too.

The *Harvard Business Review* regularly offers thoughtful articles on the process of feedback. We provide up to date links to the HBR via our website.

For further resources go to: www.coachingonthego.co.uk

Chapter 3

Being present: lift-off

Shilpa

When your body is here but your mind is elsewhere

In coaching, the concept of maintaining attention and awareness on your coachee is a fundamental skill. We call it having presence or being present. It is critical because it enables and enhances so many of the other skills that we address in this book:

- your ability to ask the best questions to evoke progress relies on presence (see Chapter 7 and Chapter 14).

- your ability to listen effectively relies on presence (see Chapter 8).

- your ability to build trust and rapport with your coachee will improve almost immeasurably with strong presence (see Chapter 5).

You can take a horse to water, but you can't make it drink

That is a way of saying that people make a lot of choices about what they do, even when you are trying to point them in a particular direction. This is absolutely true when it comes to their attention. People can simply zone out. You will have seen this. Let's face it, you probably do this yourself in a lot of meetings you attend (although hopefully not on purpose). There in body, but the mind is elsewhere.

In the English language we even speak about 'paying' attention. This is because there is a cost to attending to something because you can't attend to something else. It takes a certain amount of energy to concentrate and focus. As humans we have an energy-conserving tendency and if there is a way we can take short cuts we often do. The result is, we turn our thinking to automatic and we do not pay attention.

This may yet turn out to be the big challenge of leadership in the twenty-first century. How do you harness the vital and precious attention of people you rely on at work? They are distracted, continuously. In some cases this is frustrating, and in other cases it is downright dangerous because their mind is not on the job. There is enough research to fill several jumbo jets which consistently finds that multi-tasking reduces the quality of the output on all the tasks you are doing (see the resources section at the end of this chapter if you would like to learn more). And in case anyone is thinking it, this applies to men and women. We cannot multi-task mentally – it is a myth. While it is possible to walk and chew gum, it is not possible to have our mind consciously attending to two things.

When things get a bit uncomfortable we can zone out or get restless waiting for the difficulty to pass, and like Caroline in our story, people just want to get it over with. There are many situations in life where facing difficulty is important, for example, listening to customer feedback or dealing with angry or frustrated service-users. How do you help yourself to stay present? How do you support your team when they have to face this sort of thing? Attention is a valuable resource, and without it, all we have are empty bodies working on remote and that's not good for anyone.

Having presence is a bit like a superpower. Presence underpins 'flow', a quality that all elite athletes seek to perfect, and it is a major part of emotional intelligence. Flow describes a state when you are 'in the zone', wholly focused and immersed in your task. As a result, you are also motivated to be successful. People who are able to do this begin to see the world and situations in different ways. They scan for information in a broader manner and integrate that information in innovative ways. Like all skills, being present needs practice.

Really effective coaches know how to align their mind with their body so that they are fully present, and they also know how to help their coachee to do this as well. When both people are fully present it has a magnifying effect on the discussion. Everything is more powerful. Your role as a coach is to help people turn on their attention and awareness, to avoid habitual thinking, and most of all, to ensure that routine activity does not become automatic because opportunities get missed. So it's a double whammy. And hence double the work for you. And yet once you have this habit, the returns will fly ever higher for you, your coachees and all your colleagues.

Caroline is clearly continuing to live in the past, as we rejoin the team she is clearly not present. . .

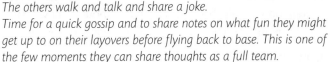

The whole flight crew has gathered as usual. Prya has welcomed everyone individually. And given one of her traditional Prya pep talks. Now, the team is walking to the departure gate. A long walk, of course, in today's modern airports and a time to catch up. Caroline is sulking, walking with eyes down and a frown. The others walk and talk and share a joke.

Time for a quick gossip and to share notes on what fun they might get up to on their layovers before flying back to base. This is one of the few moments they can share thoughts as a full team.

Implicitly, everyone understands that having a little natter and getting to know your crew mates will make life easier, but Caroline is unrelenting.

SCENE 3: THE DEPARTURE GATE

As the crew approaches the departure gate, Prya falls back slightly to allow Asif to lead them through the throng of passengers. She smiles and nods to as many passengers as she can. Asif pauses and steps up to a little girl who is beside her parents. He kneels down and, glancing first to her parents, he looks her in the eyes.

'Hi there,' he smiles. 'And who are you going to visit today?'

'We're going to see Granny and Grandad,' she answers and beams proudly.

'That's fantastic. We'll make it a super flight for you. Do come to say hello to me when we're in the air.'

Caroline, just behind, subconsciously rolls her eyes. Or at least she thought it was subconscious.

Prya meanwhile steps up to a group of passengers. 'We're so sorry that we are already so delayed here, we'll really do our best to catch up some of the time when we're flying.'

The passengers all moan about how annoying it is, and yet thank Prya for taking an interest. 'We know it's not your fault,' someone says. It only took a few moments. Prya always found it was helpful to do this. Just listening, even though there was nothing she could do, seemed to make the passengers feel better. Well most of them: 'I'm not putting up with this again. I'll fly with JumboJumbo next time', she hears one of them say.

Caroline, meanwhile, waits impatiently for the crew to finish.

Your turn at the controls

In Scene 3 above you can clearly see the power of Prya's presence. Noticing those small yet hugely important things. Caroline's lack of presence meanwhile is not having a positive effect. Indeed, unintentionally it is having a negative effect.

This coaching skill absolutely starts with you. The more you understand the power of being present and how it changes outcomes, the more you'll be able to help others achieve it too. So, in *Flying Straight and Level*, you will be the focus and in *Looping the Loop* we will move on to how you might coach others.

 FLYING STRAIGHT AND LEVEL

1. Notice when you are on automatic Pilot, when you are doing things with your body but your mind is not engaged. Typically, many of us drive in this mode – we get home and don't remember the journey.

Every time you notice you are on automatic Pilot, turn your attention to what you are doing. Make routine activities into triggers for this noticing. Here are some examples:

- Walking down the corridor to the next meeting, stop thinking about your to-do list and start noticing that you are walking. What does the corridor look like? Who is at their desk?

- Making a coffee, pause and feel your feet and smell the coffee and hear the chatter of the office. You have just stepped out of automatic.

- Sit at your desk and simply listen to the sounds that surround you. Treat it like a symphony where each sound is making a contribution – no sound is good or bad, it is simply sound. Allow all the sounds to enter your ears and note too how much you naturally screen out during a working day and how many sounds go unnoticed.

2. In three meetings next week, after 20 minutes specifically ask yourself if you are bored. And if you decide you are, turn on your laser beam of attention. Watch who speaks and who doesn't, how the topic is sent down different tributaries. Note the different ways that people have of talking to each other. Use your imagination to invent new aspects of the meeting that you can observe. Look beyond the *content* that you would normally focus on.

3. Next time you're in a meeting and you find yourself multi-tasking – checking your phone for messages or planning ahead on another project. Pause. Take three slightly deeper breaths. Say to yourself, I choose to be in this meeting. And notice if you want to say, 'I am not here by choice.' That suggests you have very little to contribute to the discussion and that you might be better to be elsewhere. Consider excusing yourself from the meeting and redeploying your time and energy. If when you say that you choose to be there, a positive flood of reactions comes up, that suggests you are right, you should be here and that is good motivation for your presence. Connect to those sensations as the meeting progresses so that you are fully engaged.

4. Stop multi-tasking. Full stop. Plenty of research confirms that multi-tasking has poor outcomes. Stop pretending to listen to a conference call while writing emails (everyone knows you are doing it – after all, you know when they do it to you). When a colleague asks to talk to you for five minutes, close down your computer and stop what you were doing. Put a poster on the wall by your desk or a note in your bag saying

'STOP multi-tasking'. Check out our resources on the research on brain capacity and brain recovery when multi-tasking.

5. Learn to be present and use Pause-Points™ (see Chapter 4).

You may find it helpful to write down your thoughts and reactions each day you practise being present.

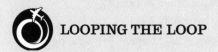 ## LOOPING THE LOOP

Do not attempt these practices until you have flown straight and level for some time.

So, how do you help others improve their ability to be present? Here are some practices you can integrate into your leadership style:

1. When you are convening meetings or conference calls, ask people to stop multi-tasking for the duration of the call or meeting.

2. You might ask meetings that you run to 'stop for a minute to think about what else we might need to discuss?' – and then have the courage to hold silence. If it helps, count silently from 0 to 10 before asking for suggestions. Silence is a great way to muster attention (see Chapter 4 where we talk about this more).

3. If you notice that others appear not to be present, address it. In a one-to-one conversation you might say, 'It feels to me that your mind is elsewhere, can I help?' or 'Something else seems to be bothering you, would it help to discuss it?' In a meeting, you might say, 'I'm noticing it's hard to concentrate at the moment, so can I suggest everyone takes a two-minute break? Or stands up and stretches? Or refreshes their coffee?'

4. Make a point of asking people questions that sharpen attention: What did you notice? What else? What did you forget to pay attention to? What haven't we thought about?

5. Ask 'feeling' questions as well as intellectual questions: How do you feel about that? What is your intuition? If you had a magic wand what would you do?

6. Last, but definitely not least, go and learn mindfulness. We've included resources that you can check out below.

THINGS TO DO BEFORE THE NEXT FLIGHT

Read Ellen J Langer's '*Mindfulness*', published in 1989 by Addison-Wesley/Addison Wesley Longman.

Read 'Mindfulness and Being Present in the Moment' in Psychology Today UK, published in January 2018.

Watch Dan Harris on YouTube talking to Googlers about Mindfulness. We provide a link on our website too.

Read 'Why smart people don't multitask' in *Entrepreneur* we provide a link through our website.

Watch Celeste Headlee 'How to Have a Good Conversation', a TEDxCreativeCoast from 2015: we provide a link on our website

For further resources go to: www.coachingonthego.co.uk

Chapter 4

Using Pause-Points™: wheels up

How stillness uncovers what's really going on

A couple of times in this book we've invited you to stop. How has that been for you? Did you manage to do it? Did you find it easy to simply stop for a moment? Welcome to the twenty-first century, the busiest time of our history.

All of us are juggling too much. That's not a criticism, it's an observation. According to MIT, the average American is spending 24 hours online per week – and the rest of the western world is not far behind.

In all this hurly burly, it is difficult to find space and silence. And yet these are precious beyond measure. At the simplest level, you may have noticed that leaders with gravitas are those that often pause before responding to a situation. They demonstrate in that small heartbeat of time that they are patiently considering options, giving due care to a question, bringing to bear all their experience on the situation. In short, they respond wisely without reacting in haste.

"Silence is the voice of mighty things."

An Old English Oak, By Hanford Lennox Gordon

Silence is often taught in negotiating courses because it is well understood that most people get anxious after more than a nanosecond of silence. In these situations, people rush to fill the silence, and this is why it is a powerful negotiating skill. The same logic applies with coaching. In general, people will fill a silence, but the intention is very different in a coaching context because we don't want to 'win' the silence, we are simply inviting our coachees to reflect and take their time.

Pause-Points™, where we hold a little silence, allow us to see what's missing, what's needed, what's best. And then decide how to act. It may be helpful for you to see space and silence as a way of inviting someone to become more present. Silence is so unusual in today's environment that it can literally shock us into alertness. Even a single beat of silence or a single breath before you answer a question or step into a conversation can make a difference. It signals to people who are listening to you that you are giving them your considered response, and when you are listening to others it signals that you are really interested to learn more.

Edgar Schein, in describing company culture talked about sedimentation, and we apply it in this context too. Thoughts, feelings, past experiences, different contexts have all sedimented within an individual. When you use Pause-Points™ and associated questions to invite your coachee to reflect, they may need to drop into these layers of sediment. We really can't stress enough to leave them space and silence to do that. You are there to bear witness to what comes up, so you need to remain present and engaged, but unobtrusively so.

Not only do Pause-Points™ signal our intention to another person, they also signal our intention to ourselves. We are inclining the mind through our pause.

Pause-Points™ are neatly sandwiched between powerful questions and listening because they often bridge between the two. However, by turning the pause into an activity we are encouraging you, and training you, to hold back. Too often coaches wait until the coachee has put the full stop on a sentence and then dive in with another question or a summary or a point of view. A full stop is a stop. Stop yourself diving in.

We use Pause-Points™ in different ways. Phil will often conclude a part of a conversation with a simple question such as 'Is there anything else?' Then he waits, and often waits a bit more. Phil says that something else always does come out, and often it is revealed to be the most salient part of the conversation. Here is the thing that they really needed to say.

This is completely in line with the experience of other professions. Doctors say that patients leaving the consulting room with their hand on the door handle often turn back and say, 'Oh, by the way. . . ' And there is nothing 'by the way' about it. This is what they really came for although they may not have realised it.

Jenny, on the other hand, often uses a Pause-Point™ at the beginning of a coaching conversation. She will invite people to stop and breathe and look inside themselves. Her favourite phrases are, 'What's *really* important for us to discuss?' or 'What's the *most important* thing here?' Again, this is followed by a good dose of space and silence. Also, at the end of a conversation, she'll suggest, 'Let's pause and consolidate the learning. What are you taking away?'

These questions help the other person to make sense of the conversation in their own way, but it also helps as a coach to hear what has really made a difference to their thinking.

With this in mind, let's rejoin the story and see how this idea of space and silence comes up here and how Pause-Points™ help.

Let's consider the issues of slot delays. Holidays are often delayed due to flights literally (well almost) fighting for the right to take off and land at their allotted times. A short delay in getting passengers and their luggage safely on board and ready for their specific slot can cause flights to drop catastrophically down the waiting list. Slot delays are hated by the crew probably more than by passengers, at least some of whom, we hope, are feeling relaxed and ready for holiday.

In our story the cabin team, in full knowledge of the consequences of a delay, are quickly getting ready to welcome everyone.

SCENE 4: GETTING READY TO FLY

Despite the rush, Tomacz takes time to check in with each head of station before popping quickly into the cockpit. 'We're just about to open up for business,' he says and flashes a winning smile. 'Anything you want to say or do before we get the passengers on the plane?'

In the midst of so much haste Prya takes time to pause. Abandoning a pre-flight checklist, she says, 'Yes. Give me two ticks.'

With a studied carefulness, she reaches up to activate the *announce* button. 'Hey everyone, I know we're late and I appreciate the backlash that you guys face when we work under these conditions. Just want to say thanks. Caroline and I will try not to add to your misery. Really great job you do for us. A big thank you to you all.'

With a flick she deactivates the button and turns back to Tomacz and says, 'Thanks for thinking to ask. Taking just a minute to recognise the team is a good investment. After all, we've got 17 hours together in this tin can.'

Caroline only listens with one ear. She can't wait to get going. Impatiently she waits for Prya to rejoin the pre-flight checks. Of course, they'd have to start from the top again. Her agitation plainly visible, Caroline starts calling each item quickly and crisply. Prya once again stops. Looks across at Caroline. And waits a moment and asks, 'Caroline? What's the matter?'

So typical of Prya to ask such a lame question, and Caroline's gut tightens once more at the possibility of an emotion-laden conversation which she instantly brushes aside. 'No. Nothing at all. I'm fine. Let's start again.'

For the third time they restart the pre-flight checks carefully dialling in settings required by the engine management system. Prya waits for Caroline to finish.

But. Then. Caroline can hold back no longer.

'Prya you're so confoundedly NICE to everyone. You bend over backwards. It's not right. You're the captain.'

'Really?' said Prya, pausing, 'I don't see it that way. I just feel very vulnerable up here. We rely on every part of the team. Imagine one nut or bolt carelessly left behind could rip the heart out of our engines. A really cross passenger having a rant back there can make the whole trip a misery for everyone.'

'When I first understood how interdependent we are up here, I found it easy and natural to think about what others needed.' She paused again. 'Oh no, listen to me. You've got me on my hobby horse again. Let's get this show on the road. Ok?'

▶

Prya smiles at Caroline and suggests, 'How about you do a welcome to the first passengers?'

As Prya had done just moments before, Caroline flips the switch and *announce* lights up.

'Good evening everyone, a very warm welcome to you all.' As she continues to explain that they're keen to catch up on lost time, she notices her resentment towards Prya softening. It surprises her to find that she genuinely feels for the passengers, if she bothers to think about it.

The size of aeroplanes these days means that it still takes another 30 minutes before all the passengers are on board. Several people have luggage that is surely bigger than they are allowed. How do they get away with it?

Caroline the Co-Pilot is at the controls. They take off perfectly and as the plane lifts into the air, so too does her mood.

Your turn at the controls

There's a lot in this chapter, so we'll point out the obvious behaviour and then spend a bit longer on the less obvious parts of the interactions. It won't have escaped your attention that Prya takes time to praise the team, and that this is in the midst of all the busy-ness. She doesn't let her focus on a narrow goal overwhelm her to the extent that she loses sight of the bigger picture: the team and the team's morale remain a priority for her.

Praise helps people to feel good about the contribution they make. Don't underestimate how much difference a little bit can make. If you've skipped Chapter 2, you may want to look back, particularly at the *Flying Straight and Level* practices, many of which include finding opportunities to praise people.

There's also a Pause-Point™ when Prya asks Caroline directly 'what's the matter?'. It's fairly common for people to brush that aside, but also common that eventually something important bursts out. It is only through pausing that Prya saw the opportunity – and this is at a time when time really does mean money.

Particularly when someone is snagged on a persistent thought or emotion, they can barge through their day trying to avoid or get rid of their discomfort. This obscuring of difficulty is a form of denial. As Caroline demonstrates, she is squashing down very powerful emotions, but in denying them, in trying to turn a blind eye to them, they are in fact dominating her and her behaviour. She is impatient, short-tempered and uncommunicative. As a leader in coaching mode, you may see a lot of this in your team. If you do see it, it signals a coaching opportunity.

Talking directly about emotions may be culturally inappropriate and, also, we don't want this to turn into therapy. But where someone is harbouring a grudge, has misinterpreted a situation or is clearly out-of-sorts with themselves or the team, you can choose to leave them to figure it out themselves (and this is a perfectly good choice). Or, you can choose to have a short coaching conversation aimed at building their self-awareness.

As an aside, you will also have noted that Prya uses a skilful device with Caroline to snap her into a new mindset. The result is that Caroline finds she can be warm and empathetic when she starts the welcome on board announcement. New perspectives are something we give more focus to in Chapter 7.

In the following behavioural experiments, we're going to explore these aspects of coaching: leaving space and silence and developing self-awareness in others.

▶

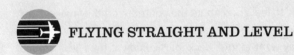 **FLYING STRAIGHT AND LEVEL**

1. Add Pause-Points™ into your everyday activities:

- Read an email, look away from the screen for a moment and notice one thing in your environment, such as smells, sights and sounds, then return to the email and compose a reply.

- Before attending an important meeting, consider what you *really* think, what you *really* want to contribute. Build space into your diary so you have time for reflection and planning. Sadly, electronic diaries allow us to book back-to-back meetings and it is easy for the day to get very full. Seize control of your diary, add in Pause-Points™, if not in your day then certainly in your week. Make a meeting with yourself and keep it as if it was a meeting with someone else. Do not use it to clear emails but to take a Pause-Point™.

- If you are sitting at your desk for a long time working intensely, take a moment to stretch. As you stretch, consider for yourself how you are, what's happening to you and if you're focusing on the right thing.

You may need a trigger to take these actions, rather than remembering it at the end of the day. Some people put alarms on their devices, others put alerts in their electronic diaries or a note or a picture on the wall in front of them. Find your own triggers as reminders. It will soon become a positive habit.

2. Consider a senior leader whom you admire. Every time you see that senior leader in action, begin to pay attention to how they use space and silence. Notice too how others react when they do take time to pause. Also, note when they do not leave space and the consequence of this behaviour.

3. Learn to get comfortable with silence. You can do that today by taking a little extra time to answer questions that others ask of you. Obviously, acknowledge that you've heard the question but indicate with your body language that you're thinking. Or simply say, 'Hmm, let me think about that' before supplying an answer. Don't overdo it. If someone asks if you want a cup of coffee, no need to stroke your chin thoughtfully as that would be really overdoing it. Otherwise, in almost any situation it is acceptable to say, 'Hold on.'

4. Keep notes of when you are too hasty in your responses. Stop every now and again and think through where you could have paused and what consequence that might have had.

5. Praise yourself when you do add some space. Again, notice what happens when you do this. Even though you may still be mastering this, noting when you do and don't manage to take a Pause-Point™ will heighten your awareness for the next time.

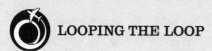

LOOPING THE LOOP

1. When talking one to one with others, start using Phil's phrase, 'Is there anything else?' and leaving space for people to genuinely reflect.

2. Find other phrases that you feel comfortable using that invite people to drill down further inside themselves, to give non-habitual answers. Here are some examples:

- How do you see things?
- Where is your energy on this right now?
- Go deeper on that and tell me what is underneath your comments.
- Say more.
- Help me understand that point better.

Remember, there really is no hurry when you ask these questions and the more unsure the coachee is about what's happening, the longer it will take for them to find the right words or the courage to express it to you. The quickest way for you to stop them reflecting is to get impatient or to jump into the silence yourself.

And if you receive a reply that sounds like 'What do you mean?' respond with: 'Whatever comes to mind?' And pause again to allow your coachee to consider their answer.

3. Have confidence that these Pause-Points™ will unlock the coachee's understanding of themselves and the situation. With this confidence, start adding a gentle silence. Note that we use gentle silence because we have been in situations where silence is used as a form of 'blink' – who's going to speak first. Rather, in this context, the silence is indicating they should take their time, there's no rush, and it's important they speak about whatever is important for them.

▶

4. And if you worry that the silence is too long, that's completely normal. Phil was always the talkative extrovert, so this silence is not easy. He still has to quieten his inner voice when leaving the longer silences for his coachees. And it works. So, expect to feel uncomfortable. Just keep practising.

5. For the next week, consider all the meetings that you will lead and deliberately design in some Pause-Points™. How will you do that? What is culturally appropriate? How can you help others to understand that this is a deliberate practice and you haven't got a screw loose?

6. Finally, we rarely suggest what **not** to do. Yet sometimes people ask if it's okay to count in your head as a way to stop you from filling the silence before the coachee. We encourage you to practise to see what happens. And yet the risk here is that while counting in your head your attention is drawn away from your coachee. Try holding the silence in your head and focus your listening on the coachee in anticipation of their next words.

7. Practise some in-situ mindfulness. While you wait for the kettle to boil, while you brush your teeth or while you walk down the corridor, turn your mind fully to what you are doing. Don't multi-task.

THINGS TO DO BEFORE THE NEXT FLIGHT

Read Edgar Schein's work.

Read Tim Parks' novel *'Teach Us to Sit Still: A Sceptic's Search for Health and Healing'* about learning to meditate, published in 2010 by Random House.

Read Nancy Kline's *'Time to Think: Listening to Ignite the Human Mind'* published in 1999 by Hachette UK.

Watch Nancy Kline's ideas on YouTube.

Watch a meditation by Jon Kabat Zinn

We provide links to Schein, Kline and Kabat-Zinn on our website along with further resources, go to: www.coachingonthego.co.uk

Chapter 5

Building trust and rapport: soaring high

On being human at work

Prya, who has been perfect beyond belief in our story so far, is about to demonstrate that even clever people can do silly things.

The point is that she is showing her human side. In different cultures around the world, and in different companies, this may be met with varying degrees of acceptance or nausea. The Brits are famously squeamish about the American fondness for over-familiarity, and you should see the Germans when faced with the in-your-face-casualness of the Antipodeans! We're not stereotyping, merely acknowledging that cultural differences exist.

Yet, against those cultural differences, there is a universal truth: that people relate to people and many jobs expect us to be personable and sometimes it's that extra step just a little beyond professional. So, showing an appropriate amount of your human side is important, as is finding your personal style where you are comfortable with the blending of professional and friendly.

This also raises the question of vulnerability. Depending on your personal beliefs about leadership, you may hold on to a view that leaders need to be strong and invincible. You may think that leaders never admit to making an error of judgement or showing an emotion. What you do, needs to be authentic to you and culturally appropriate. But. Everyone is a boss watcher, so if you don't share the real you, your team and peers are unlikely to share the real them.

Why is this important, you may ask? First, because effective coaching means creating an environment where the coachees can confidently share their innermost feelings and thoughts with you (if they choose to). A coachee will find this easier the greater the trust and rapport they have with you. And second, because coaching often relies on you understanding someone's real motivations. We encourage you to be really, really, curious about what they want out of life and their job. If secretly they want to be a great novelist, well that's good to know. Now you understand the limits and opportunities of their commitment to the job. Clearly, they're going to thrive if you can find ways to align that ambition with tasks or projects that present themselves within the workplace.

So, getting back to you and how much of yourself you disclose. People appreciate knowing the real you, not just the cardboard cut-out of you. You don't need to be over-familiar or reveal things that make you uncomfortable, but you will struggle to build trusting and confidential relationships if you're not prepared to reveal a little bit of the private you.

What is rapport?

We see rapport as being the sense of connection that you have with someone. Good rapport is like being in sync with someone, where you are mutually interested in each other and often hold congruent emotions. As a leader and as a coach, being in rapport with each person individually shows that you respect and recognise their very individuality. As such, authenticity is key.

In Part 3: The Pilot's manual, we consider some more challenging methods to improve your ability to build rapport. Here we stick to some of the basics which can be easily overlooked. Phil remembers a highly experienced colleague who once accused him of creating a bad impression by dressing inappropriately at work. He was told he should never wear jeans on a normal workday at the office. As it happens, Phil is absolutely certain he had not worn jeans, but the colleague was convinced. In this, and many other situations, what matters is the colleague's perception as it clearly affected his rapport.

Diversity and inclusion

To the extent that you successfully and effectively share your human side while at the same time enabling your coachees to do the same, you are smack-bang in the centre of issues of diversity and inclusion. If, especially as a leader, you have considered this to be a side issue to your working life, it's time to change.

Most companies these days have very good diversity and inclusion policies and many companies go to considerable lengths to hold workshops on unconscious bias and other habits we have that can lead to exclusionary behaviours. Despite these policies, we have found ourselves coaching around issues of 'the personal' in the workplace. These may be issues of race, gender, sexuality or neuro-diversity. If, for example, your company has a culture where teams socialise outside work hours, this can come up. Or if in your industry sales people entertain customers, that can come up. And if you and your team are working with clients in intimate settings, maybe such as healthcare or even an airline, where does common human-ity stop and inappropriate personal revelation begin?

Just to illustrate these ideas in more detail, we've found ourselves coaching around the following situations:

- Single women who don't like to entertain male clients but know that if they were a man they would do it, and that the industry expects this level of familiarity.

- Gay guys who find the after-work drink with their workmates includes gentle badinage which makes them feel uncomfortable and exaggerates their differences from the heterosexual team.

- Neuro-diverse individuals who fail to 'read' a social work situation and make inappropriate remarks and jokes which offend others who are present.

- People on an international assignment who don't want high levels of familiarity in the work situation and are seen as overly formal and aloof.

- Work situations where it is usual for the spouse to help with entertain-ing senior visitors, but the spouse is unavailable or uninterested.

- Individuals in the caring professions who talk about their own struggles as a way to build empathy and rapport, knowing that as they do so they are walking a very fine – and grey line – in their professional code of conduct.

- A single parent who can never make the breakfast sessions which are run to encourage networking across the industry because they must do the school run.

When you and your team face any of these situations, or any similar situ-ations, this signals a definite opportunity to use coaching to move issues forward. You cannot tell someone how to be friendly, but as a leader you do need to tell them where the boundaries are and help them figure out their own way to be authentic and human.

If you are going to coach around these issues, you absolutely have to know your company's diversity and inclusion policy, as well as the client entertainment policy. So get a copy and read them, and then examine your own assumptions about this subject. Think about how you show your human side and how you have learnt to do this authentically.

Let's see how Prya is building trust and rapport.

SCENE 5: OFF THEY GO

With Caroline in charge, Prya takes the opportunity to make another announcement. She loves this part of her job and really can't help turning into a little bit of a show-off.

'Hi there everyone, this is Prya your Pilot speaking. We're really sorry for the delay so far. Caroline is our first officer and Asif our second officer and we're all up front here taking shifts overnight. We're having a competition as to who can be the most grumpy about the delay. Unfortunately, we all love flying too much so that failed. Have you ever noticed how sunny it is once we're above the clouds? Up here it is always blue skies. Anyway, because we took off late and we know that is a really bad start to your holiday, we'll radio ahead and try to do a deal to move forward our landing slot. The best motivation I can think of is the threat that we all sing Yellow Submarine. Everyone, you might want to practise the chorus back there?'

Henrik in the cabin could sense the passengers smiling inwardly and some of them smiling openly. One or two even started

▶

singing. He loved it when the Pilots helped the team like this. Prya continued, 'We will also make sure that we will pedal extra fast on our route today and with any luck we will catch up the lost time.'

I wish their jokes would improve. Not sure I need to add anything. A meal is being served – it could be dinner, it could be lunch. Having just complained about Prya's jokes, I'll make airline food quips later.

The lights are dimmed to encourage sleep – even though no one is quite sure what time zone this fits!!

Your turn at the controls

We know of at least three airlines that use the personal touch as a point of differentiation. One that Jenny knows well showed an in-flight safety briefing with the crew naked. Clever camera angles preserved the crew's modesty. Another airline allegedly interviewed Pilots in Hawaiian shorts and shirt and expected them to tell jokes (we haven't verified whether this is fact but it has entered urban legend). And yet a further airline has a range of celebrities parodying themselves to help to get the message across. These examples point to some situations requiring a more personal approach, a lightness of touch and this, of course can be difficult for some people. Not everyone wears flowery shirts with ease.

Nevertheless, airlines, the hospitality and entertainment industries, sales functions and business deal-making are just some examples of situations where individuals become the friendly face of the business. Even when the job spec is very clear that 'personality' or 'an outgoing nature' are important, you may find someone in your team who has deep technical skills and struggles with some of the personal aspects of the job. Or you may have an introvert who doesn't like to socialise. For these people, the personal side of professional can be difficult.

You need to become comfortable with your personal style. How do you admit mistakes, show you are vulnerable, express care for your team and generally show that you are human too? No one will confide in you if you seem like a heartless robot. So, take off that coat of armour and let's look at what you can try.

 FLYING STRAIGHT AND LEVEL

1. Try to be human. This starts with a bit of self-enquiry.

Ask yourself how you demonstrate that you're human. Consider the following:

- Without acting the fool, how do I encourage people to laugh and have fun at work?
- When I make a mistake, how do I acknowledge it?
- How do I make each member of my team feel special and cared for?
- If someone asked my team, my peers or my boss whether they trust me, what's my best guess about the response?

Your answers will tell you how you're doing at being human and we expect them to identify gaps so that you can see what else you might do to be more human. Start these now.

If these seem like easy questions to answer, then we have not quite succeeded. We anticipate that answering these should take a good period of reflection. Identify examples for each question to justify and illustrate your answers. Think separately about each person in your team (the one that you are in as well as the one you lead).

2. On building rapport, try these out. They are all easy and yet they require attention at first to be sure you are doing them reliably and ▶

you need to evaluate whether they are culturally appropriate in each occasion:

- Dress consistently with your environment. Can you adjust in the moment? For example, remove a tie and potentially acknowledge the point openly, 'I seem to have overdressed for this occasion. My apologies. I'll get it right next time.'

- Remember and use people's names.

- Don't overstay your welcome. If you asked for 15 minutes of someone's time, check if it is Okay after 15 minutes if you would like more.

- Observe others you are meeting glancing at their watch and ask them directly if you need to wrap up soon.

- Identify a colleague with whom you've not got a good relationship, and invite them for coffee to get to know each other better.

- Use some small talk at the start of a conversation, by asking how someone is feeling. To do this genuinely, you need to listen and respond to the answer, draw in what they said previously or link it to other factors: 'I remember you said last time that issues with your father were making it hard to concentrate, so how are you doing today?' Gauging how much small talk to use is another skill to hone because we know people who annoyingly waste a good ten minutes on these niceties. So, practise them and reflect.

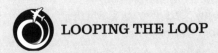 **LOOPING THE LOOP**

1. A technique that has wide applications in coaching and can help build trust and rapport is that of appreciative inquiry (also known as AI, although there is nothing artificial about it). It is a powerful questioning technique and demonstrates your focus on the coachee rather than yourself, which builds rapport. Appreciative inquiry is a technique that deliberately sidesteps what does not work. Rather it focuses on identifying what is working well, analysing why it is working well and then doing more of it. Doing more of the positive is a way to address what does not work.

2. Appreciative inquiry is a way of helping your coachee find a parallel situation and apply their insights from that situation to the one they are exploring with you. In the context of helping a coachee improve their own rapport-building capabilities, you might try the following:

- Can you remember a time when you did enjoy being personal or getting to know your colleagues or a client and it had a good outcome? What were the features of that situation? What might transfer across another situation?'

- Have you seen someone else build rapport really well? Someone you admire. What do they do that seems to make it so successful? What might you try that is authentic to your personality?

- When have you built a great relationship with someone very quickly? What did you do then?

3. Some people are held back from being personal because they think that it is going to slide even further and become invasively personal, and that scares them or upsets them. In which case helping them to have some simple coping strategies can help. You might try asking:

- When you've been in this situation before and you've felt uncomfortable, what happened? What did you do? If you had a magic wand and you could re-engineer that situation what would your magic wand wish had happened? What coping strategy does that help you think about?

- What coping devices can you come up with that will help you feel that you are really in control? What will help you feel that this is really on your terms?

- If someone makes an inappropriate remark – whether to you directly or generally – what form of words will you use to signal that it makes you uncomfortable? What other words might you use? What actions might you take if it continues?

4. Also, don't forget to reassure people that they can absolutely find their own way and their own solutions and that being friendly can be done by introverts too. They don't have to sing to a crowded plane.

THINGS TO DO BEFORE THE NEXT FLIGHT

An entertaining book that includes very useful memory techniques to help you remember names and other facts is Derren Brown's *'Tricks of the Mind'*, published by Channel 4. It also includes some interesting discussions on bias.

Read this article in *Harvard Business Review* 'The Neuroscience of Trust' and check out the link we provide on our website.

Watch a TED Talk on trust, go to our website for the link.

For further resources go to: www.coachingonthego.co.uk

Chapter **6**

Creating awareness: facing air turbulence

What to do when someone isn't seeing clearly

We would love to think our minds are like a judge in court taking on board all the facts and weighing up the evidence before coming to a well-considered conclusion. Or that our mind is clear enough to create accurate memories like photographs. Not true. The evidence is that our minds are much more like a lawyer, selective and deliberately emphasising facts and events that support our pre-established narrative. We see what we want or expect to see and we select facts that fit our pre-built story. This is called 'confirmation bias'. One of the roles of a coach is to assist their coachee in overcoming such biases.

In the next instalment of our story you will see that Caroline is falling into this trap. She is inaccurately finding evidence to suit her belief that she should be promoted and ignoring the other stuff, which ironically would help her achieve this very goal. Her inability to listen and her unconscious selection of facts allows her to believe that she has been unjustly treated.

Given that there is so much academic evidence that humans just won't change their minds when they are presented with facts, it may cause you to call into question the value of coaching. After all, what's the point of coaching someone if they're just not open to change? This is why self-awareness is so very important, and the key word here is 'self'. Just as no individual has the power to motivate everyone, nor can you present facts to a person to develop their self-awareness. They need to find the 'ah ha' themselves. Things only change when they see the change. Awareness and self-awareness are necessary precursors to change.

Jenny was once told: 'People **accept** the conclusions of others; they can only **act** on their own conclusions.' This is why self-awareness is so vital: the awareness is generated by the coachee and they will now act upon it.

To build self-awareness, team leaders and organisations often turn to psychometric tests where the team members each complete a questionnaire and a professional, trained to analyse the tests, provides a map of each person's characteristics and how each person matches or differs from others in the team. You may have used these tests yourself or been in teams where you completed them. Examples are MBTI, Firo-B and Primary Colours. This is one way, but not the only way, to start the process of awareness building. In Part 3: The Pilot's manual, we provide ideas and guidance on how you might best use these tools.

Sometimes, however, people can feel pigeon-holed or labelled by these psychometric tests, which can have unintended negative effects. Hence, we prefer to focus on a range of ways you can coach people to know themselves better, and to realise the impact that they're having on others and on the situation they're facing. We think the learning for you and your coachees can be significantly more impactful.

We also need to consider when an individual is being wilfully blind. Although the term 'wilful blindness' originated in legal circles, it is a feature of the modern workplace and workplace relationships. It means that someone is deliberately (subconsciously or otherwise) avoiding considering how their action or inaction contributes to an outcome. It could be an outcome they desire both individually and organisationally. Without awareness, personal adaptation is programmatic, compliance-driven and lifeless. With awareness a person can transform almost instantly.

We have seen coachees make radical adjustments to their attitude and approach once they have gained some insight into themselves. Examples include:

- Phil, an ex-finance director and extremely comfortable with facts and figures, began to see how issues of relationship might be just as important to the success of the business.

- A perpetually angry employee coming to see how they played a role in creating the very situations that made them mad.

- A lazy team member who came to the realisation that they were focusing on entirely the wrong things in their job, re-oriented their priorities and became a human dynamo.

- A team member who wanted promotion realising that they didn't actually want the extra responsibility and that their current job could be entirely satisfactory for their lifestyle choices.

Creating awareness can be extraordinarily simple and yet it regularly requires your intervention as a coach. Your action simply draws attention to something – and not always something that you as the coach (or boss) are aware of. Phil recalls a senior management consultant saying, 'Until you asked me how I bring into the workplace the creativity that runs through the activities in my personal life, I had never thought of them as having any connection. And yet they should. Why do I deny my desire to be creative when I come to work? This can change everything for me.'

Repeating and summarising

Another way to enable awareness is to help your coachee hear their own words or how you, the listener, understood their words. These steps can have a significant impact by drawing attention to what might otherwise be part of a bigger whole.

REPEATING

The most powerful technique can be to repeat back exactly what your coachee said, taking care to emphasise either what you heard or what you think they meant, often with a raised intonation creating a question: 'So, promotion is the most important thing'?' You might pick on a single word 'promotion'?

When you repeat, you use their words and stick to their point of view. This triggers your coachee to consider the significance of their chosen words. And hence their accuracy. Which builds their awareness.

Repeating is a mirror. You are striving for accuracy to the original sense that's been expressed.

SUMMARISING

When you summarise, you use your own words and your understanding to check that you are both aligned. Your aim is to share a summary of your understanding of what was said in your own words, probably the most important aspects. It may be helpful to indicate that you are seeking to change their words but deliver the same message: 'In my words, I heard you say that nothing whatsoever, including your family and your health, is as important to you as gaining promotion this year.'

This gives your coachee the opportunity to agree or disagree. To establish nuances and gain clarity. To gain awareness.

Changes in awareness can be incremental or revelatory, requiring reflection and time. Although this next chapter in our story hasn't got any instant transformations, let's see what happens with Caroline's awareness (or continuing self-delusion) before offering you some techniques to develop yours and your coachees.

Caroline meets Anja, another crew member, in the kitchen area as she makes her way to the in-flight beds. Shilpa, her colleague, is busy making coffee for someone.

SCENE 6: GOING TO SLEEP

'What's the matter?' enquires Anja 'You looked really unhappy at the team briefing.'

'Oh nothing. I'm tired.'

'Tired?'

'Yes. Tired of this whole situation.'

'And?' asks Anja.

'I just think it's unfair. I'm sure I'm good enough for a promotion, but FC and the panel don't think so.'

'Really' says Anja.

'Yes. I just had my discussion with FC this morning and he says I'm not ready.'

Anja remains silent and inclines her head towards Caroline.

'I don't know what I'm doing wrong. I think they're blaming me for the incident in Istanbul.'

'What's your evidence for that?' asks Anja.

'Why else would they not promote me? It's so unfair.'

Again, Anja remains silent.

'Okay, so I suppose I have no evidence at all that they are blaming me for Istanbul. But what else could it be?'

Anja waits.

'FC said something about demonstrating I am part of the whole team. Something about supporting others and engaging more with the passengers.'

'And how's that going?' asks Anja.

'Well, I could probably do more.'

'Do more?'

'Yes. Well, I noticed Prya chatting to passengers in the terminal. Maybe I should do more of that?'

'That sounds like a great idea' Anja enthuses. 'When might you start doing it?'

Caroline looks at Anja, smiles softly, nods her head slowly, turns around and walks up to the nearest group of passengers enjoying a coffee.' Hi there, how's it going so far at this end of the plane?'

Your turn at the controls

Caroline isn't the most self-aware person in the story and you might have someone like her that you work with. Helping people to become more aware is one of the most impactful outcomes of coaching, as it has lasting effect and huge consequences.

Caroline is demonstrating a small dollop of wilful blindness, determined to see the Istanbul incident (whatever that was) as the cause of her promotion failure. In fact, the truth is that other aspects of her behaviour are having a far bigger effect on her prospects. She is demonstrating a frustrating mix of both lack of awareness and denial. Here are some things you might try if you face this situation.

 FLYING STRAIGHT AND LEVEL

1. Anja does the basics very skilfully in the scene above. She simply uses single words as a form of repeating to indicate she's listening and adds a question mark: Tired? And? She's also using Pause-Points™ to help.

   Combined with comfortable silence, this is a natural way to encourage people to be more introspective, or to simply spell out what they really mean. These single words that mirror back to the coachee their words are more than just a 'hhmm' for example, which might simply mean that you are listening. But repeating a key word means you are ready to understand. That takes the conversation to a whole new level.

   If you're not entirely convinced of this, maybe it sounds too easy or too superficial, play a game this next week simply cueing into people's statements. Use the one-word question technique and see what they say. Target doing this, say, 14 times. (Why 14 times and not 10, 12 or 15? 14 is a more unusual number so you're more likely to recall the practice and do it.) ▶

2. In every other meeting for the next two weeks, look for an opportunity to check in with somebody regarding what they have just said. This will increase your understanding and it will also improve your colleague's understanding of the issues. Use these phrases to help you start, and then find your own:

- What I heard you say is. . .
- If I could summarise that, you think. . .
- If I might paraphrase, you said. . .
- Using my own words, I think you're saying that. . .

3. When you're ready, start challenging yourself to ask more powerful questions designed to motivate your coachee to see how they are showing up and increase their self-awareness. You might ask:

- How are you contributing to this impasse?
- What's your role in creating this situation?
- What's clear to you and what's not clear to you?
- Where could it be down to you and where could it be down to others?
- Or use Anja's question: What evidence do you have for that?

4. An excellent technique to create awareness is to ask your coachee to score or rank the issue and then explore that position:

- On a scale of 0 to 10 where 0 is the lowest possible and 10 the highest: How angry are you? How important is this to you? How far have you to go on this journey?
- Responding to their answer: What makes it a [five]? What would make you change your mind? What would make it higher? [or lower?]

5. In all cases, whenever your coachee comes up with a positive solution or a positive step forward be sure to use a closing question, such as: When might you start doing that? Based on that insight, what will you do next? How can you now positively progress the situation?

These types of question have the effect of binding intention to action and they are useful in all sorts of situations. Guiding your coachee to their next action is a core part of coaching.

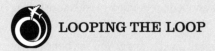

LOOPING THE LOOP

A slightly more advanced tool for helping to build awareness is called 'naming', as in naming what you see. *Naming* is a way of pointing to behaviour and its consequence and allowing your coachee to say how they see it. Naming is a back and forth activity between you both until you have found an acceptable description (the name) that you both recognise and that is sitting behind the resulting actions. It has four primary steps, although you may iterate between them and find they are not all necessary.

To help you get the gist of it, here are a few examples of naming that Anja could have used in the previous scene with Caroline:

1. Start with an opening phrase to frame the conversation:

- There's something happening here that deserves our attention.
- Something's not quite right, can we talk about it?
- I can't be sure what it is, but something has come up that we need to clear up.

Freely use the word *'something'* at this point because it indicates that you're not exactly sure what it is and it shows you are curious to find out. 'Something' is a marvellous way to open a discussion without it feeling like finger-pointing or blame. It also avoids a shopping list of woes as it is asking for specifics without limiting it to just one thing.

2. Next, try a tentative naming, again leaving room for improvement and inviting their point of view. Your job is not to find a perfect name at this point as you are simply trying to start off in a neutral way. You might start with a statement such as:

- It seems to me that you're at an impasse.
- It seems to me that you are angry.
- It seems to me that you are hugely disappointed.
- What I notice is that you keep going back to Istanbul.

You may now find that using a Pause-Point™ and leaving a gentle silence results in your coachee naming the dynamic as they see it. If Caroline was a bit more self-aware, she might say, 'Hmmm, now you mention it, ▶

I think my pride is hurt', 'It's less about disappointment and more feeling like an imposter' or 'I feel like I've let myself down'.

These statements or namings are all good to know. You can honestly say thank you and then move the coaching conversation on from there.

However, we're going to assume that Caroline wasn't that forthcoming, so there's a bit more work to do to get the naming right.

3. Invite your coachee directly to name it:

- What's behind this?
- What's the upset?
- What's going on for you right now?
- How do you see it?
- How are you feeling?

You will generally find people open up, they investigate their feelings and they find assumptions that are uninspected. Your job at this point is to listen, ask more questions and remember that the coachee needs to do the work and you are not here to fix them.

4. Self-awareness develops as the coachee speaks. But you truly help them see what's been happening when you summarise with a *when/then* statement. If the first three steps do not appear to have created more awareness and you have noticed something (again, *something*) that might help – you can add this final step.

In the story so far, the when/then statement could be one of the following (pick one and wait to see if it resonates):

- **When** you get angry, **then** you tend to lash out at others as if it is their fault.
- **When** things aren't going your way, **then** you seem to withdraw from the team.
- **When** FC gave you feedback, **then** you stopped listening.
- **When** you start blaming others, **then** you lose the opportunity to learn.
- **When** you feel criticised, **then** you start retaliating.
- **When** you don't get what you think you deserve, **then** you seem to tell yourself you don't care, when really you do.

Your coachee may amend the when/then statement or develop it further in order to express how it feels and appears to them. This is okay if it helps them gradually see what was otherwise hidden to them.

(When/then is also a feedback technique. See Chapter 2)

Think of opportunities when you might have used this naming technique in the last two weeks. Reflect back over the recent past and consider what you might have said. Next, as you end each of the next three weeks, spend ten minutes seeing if you can identify situations in which you could test this technique out in the coming week – and do so.

THINGS TO DO BEFORE THE NEXT FLIGHT

Watch a funny example of summarising and repeating on YouTube; our website provides a link.

Familiarise yourself with the Johari window (see Part 3: The Pilot's manual).

Read Freddie Strasser and Paul Randolph's *'Mediation: A Psychological Insight into Conflict Resolution'* published in 2004 by A&C Black.

For further resources go to: www.coachingonthego.co.uk

Chapter 7

Changing perspective: admiring the view from 35,000 feet

Why seeing differently creates change naturally

One aspect of being human is a tendency to suffer from *premature cognitive commitment*. Premature cognitive commitment means that we get a bit of tunnel vision and start seeing things 'one' way and only one way.

Businesses do this a lot, and corporate history is littered with organisations who have failed to see that the market is changing or that their product is about to be overtaken. Although some of them have struggled on, do you remember the giants of Kodak and Nokia and Blackberry - at one time they all dominated their industries, yet failed to see subtle early signs of change. Although these might be seen as failures in corporate strategy, the principle is the same. When thinking is fixed and rigid it constrains our abilities to adapt.

We do this with people, situations and objects. People are categorised into those we like, think are smart, funny, demanding, scary and so on. Situations are categorised as challenging, difficult, dangerous, fun, wonderful, relaxing, awe-inspiring and so on. All the stuff in our lives is categorised.

Creating categories is an evolutionary adaptation because it reduces the workload of the brain, so we're not saying it is always a bad thing. It becomes limiting when the categories are overly fixed and this is why a new perspective can be helpful. Our words can restrict thinking - new subheading.

When you, your colleagues, stakeholders, sponsors or political masters use language that is definite then this will reinforce a tendency towards automatic and unquestioning acceptance of information. This is mindlessness. When absolute language is used it subtly frames statements so that people feel reassured that they know what's going to happen. Expressions such as 'in my view,' 'what I notice is,' and 'it seems to me' remind us that there are different ways to see things. When we use absolute language, such as 'This is the problem' or 'They don't get it', we create the illusion that the problem has a single analysis and a single path to resolution. On the other hand, conditional language helps prompt a wider set of viewpoints.

A lot of coaching is helping people to see things in a new way – to gain a new perspective.

Seeing a situation through a new lens is challenging but often very achievable. Seeing a person through a new lens can be more difficult. We seem to be very quick to categorise people and then keep our opinions very fixed.

This can be a problem particularly for teams who have senior stakeholders who seem to get the reputation for being difficult and that reputation can then stick. Ultimately, individuals can end up framing their interactions with certain stakeholders through this lens. It is difficult to imagine that this situation is conducive to them doing their best work or building successful working relationships. Hence, it can take longer and require greater coaching skills to help a coachee adjust their perspective of another person.

When considering which stakeholders may be relevant to your coachee, the Up, Down and Around™ model, can be a useful guide (see the figure below). The main principle behind this is drawing a coachee's attention to the different parties they manage at work, including themselves. As an aside, it can be useful to ask coachees how much time they spend at work in each of these areas and how useful or effective that is. Here, it can be used to ask your coachee to identify all the different parties they manage as a first step to considering the different perspectives of those parties.

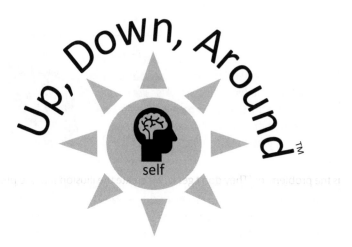

The Up Down and Around model

Finally, professional coaches often use a technique known as 'perceptual positions'. You can easily use it too and we explain how in the final *Looping the Loop* activity below as it can feel more challenging to many people. It uses the basis of up to five different perceptual positions that exist for everyone, through which life is experienced: seen, understood, felt, smelt, touched:

- 1st position – from your own perspective

- 2nd position – from a specific other person's perspective

- 3rd position – from an objective outsider's perspective

- 4th position – from the system's (or systems') perspective of which you are a part

- 5th position – from a universal, religious or spiritual perspective

And now back to the story as two new characters join us to discuss Caroline's fate.

Shilpa likes this part of the flight best. The passengers are fed and mostly quiet. Sleeping, reading or watching films. And kids are playing computer games knowing their exhausted parents won't stop them. It is a time to clear up, an opportunity to relax a little and a chance to reflect.

Shilpa is feeling preoccupied. She is having trouble at home as her parents and her partner's parents are struggling in their old age. In addition, her four teenage children are, well, being teenage children. Nonetheless, when Henrik turns to her she senses her full attention is needed. She quickly shuts out those other thoughts to focus on him. She looks him in the eye, relaxes her face and opens her ears fully.

SCENE 7: A DIFFERENT VIEW?

Henrik comes to sit next to her and asks, 'Have you got a moment for a private chat?'

Shilpa nods and smiles – she'd have time to consider her own thoughts later. 'Sure, I've got five minutes unless a passenger calls.'

'What's up with Caroline? I heard on the grapevine she crashed and burned in her discussion with FC.'

'I don't know,' replies Shilpa, 'How does she seem to you?'

'Well, it's a mixture. She seemed annoyed with Prya chatting to the passengers as usual and was cross when Tomacz interrupted their pre-flight checks. On the other hand, I just saw her cheering up some of the passengers.'

Shilpa pauses and asks, 'What do you think it must be like to be in her shoes?'

To be honest, part of Henrik was hoping for some salacious gossip, but Shilpa's question was a good one. 'It's got to be tough. Prya is such a great person. She just embodies everything in the leadership manual, if there is one. And the corporate values. It's a lot for someone who still has stuff to learn. I think I would find it hard sometimes. FC has a reputation for having the tough conversations. I know he's equally fierce about support-ing our development but, wow, the honesty of his appraisals are something else.'

Shilpa stays quiet. It feels like an age before Henrik speaks again, although it probably wasn't.

'I guess I would be a bit uncertain for a while in her shoes, but hopefully I would notice and learn from the good things around me. And, I'd hope for support from my friends and colleagues while trying to adjust. Work's got to be fun, otherwise it would be hell around here. You've only got to think about the terri-ble reputation the staff have at JumboJumbo airlines. You can

▶

see their smiles have been pre-painted! Maybe we should do something to let Caroline know we're with her all the way?'

'Good idea,' says Shilpa and continues, 'And remember, it wasn't so long ago you had to do some of your own course-correction. When we feel down, a bit of compassion is really appreciated.'

At that moment a passenger's head appears around the curtain. 'How can we help you?' asked Henrik.

Your turn at the controls

Before we dive into how to help people develop new perspectives, we're going to pause and review a few other features of the conversation between Shilpa and Henrik. We trust by now you're getting wise to our ways. You may have noted the following:

- Henrik does a tiny bit of contracting: 'Have you got a moment for a private chat?' and Shilpa responds: 'Sure, I've got five minutes. . . '

- Shilpa makes sure she is fully present for their chat.

- Shilpa is unafraid of silence and allows space to enter the discussion.

- She also asks great questions: 'How does she seem to you?'

The most important thing that Shilpa does is ask a question designed to invite a new perspective: 'What do you think it must be like to be in her shoes?'

Below you'll find some more ideas to help you practise this.

FLYING STRAIGHT AND LEVEL

1. The easiest way to get started is to note when you or others are stuck in one point of view and then to ask, 'How else could we see this? Who would have a different view?'

2. Catch yourself using definite language: 'It is this way', or 'I know how they think', or 'we *must* do the following'. Start changing your language to use words such as *maybe, probably, likely, possibly, often, sometimes*.

3. Explain the psychological process of premature cognitive commitment to your colleagues and invite them to point out to you when you fall prey to this habit of mind.

4. Another way to help develop awareness is by actively encouraging someone to consider another point of view. Some people find it helpful to write and others just to talk it through. Others might want to draw a picture (see Part 3: The Pilot's manual, for more on using visual metaphors in coaching). You decide what's right for the coachee and tailor these suggestions depending on the natural orientation of the other person.

   • Ask them to write down the counter-argument to their current thinking.

   • Ask them to draw out the links between what they think and the actions they are taking and how others might see it.

   • Ask them to describe how another stakeholder might see the situation.

   • Invite them to go and visit a customer, supplier or contractor or agency to get another point of view. Then suggest they present what they learnt to the rest of the team.

 LOOPING THE LOOP

In this section we're going to provide a couple of ideas for you to help someone else re-evaluate their judgement of an important stakeholder. We assume that it will be beneficial to your coachee and their work outcomes for this stakeholder relationship to improve, and we also assume that the ▶

stakeholder in question is hierarchically more senior and currently, perfectly ambivalent to the situation. Finally, we assume that your coachee has sought guidance on this issue. If not, and you are the boss, you will need to be aware of *phoney-coaching* which we address in the Pilot's manual.

1. Start your coaching at a time and place where you are not rushed. Contracting skills will improve the impact you have. This is a conversation that is less *On-the-Go* and more at its own pace.

   Start by asking for your coachee's evaluation of the relationship. Use an open question and neutral language so that you are not imposing your judgements: How is your relationship with xyz? What's your sense of how abc views our department, the project or our team? How well do you get on with abc?'

   People are motivated to work on different aspects of a relationship when they become aware of the impact it is having on something they care about. Therefore, the next thing to ask about is, what impact this is having on a relationship and what might a better relationship mean for the outcomes of the department, team or project. If your assessment of the relationship is correct, then you could ask how that might be getting in the way of them having the influence they want, how it could be damaging to you, them and the project, how it might be holding you back and what it's stopping you achieving.

   At this point it is natural to collude with ther assessment, but it is a mistake to do so. Also, it is a mistake to give your own or a different assessment. Although it may feel absolutely the right thing to do, these two types of remarks can lead you into a gossip session. Or, you are left debating about whose assessment is the most accurate. So, much better to simply stay with what your coachee sees and experiences.

   Now you have an assessment of the status quo and its impact, you can establish what the potential is. Ask about an aspirational future state (note, avoid evaluating whether it's achievable at this point). Ask one of these, for example: 'If you had a magic wand, what elements of the relationship would you change? What impact could that have? If this was the best working relationship possible, what would it look like? What could you achieve working together in this way? What might be possible if abc was a positive advocate for us, you or the project?'

This series of questions has established the size of the gap: where the relationship is now, where it could be and the lost opportunity of avoiding these relationship issues. In short, you have asked your coachee to build a case for change.

Case for change established, now you need to help your coachee develop relationship-building strategies. Here are some ideas to help you do that:

- Use appreciative inquiry to find positive examples that can be transferred to this situation (See Chapter 5).

- Use a fantasy question to help them think more creatively: 'If this was your very best friend and you discovered that things weren't good between you, what might you do?'

- Ask a question from the future: 'If you were 15 years older looking back on this relationship, what would you say to yourself? What would you say to abc?'

- Ask a question that evokes empathy and a softening of attitude. For example, you might make up a scenario to see how a different perspective might change things: 'If you knew that abc worked tirelessly at weekends, during holidays and after work for a children's charity and was responsible for providing help to some of the most vulnerable people in our society, how might that change things between you?'

2. A variation on the technique above, often called 'perceptual positions', is used by many professional coaches. And you can use this too. The key is to identify any relevant positions with your coachee, personify them and then have your coachee literally 'step into' being that person to describe their perspective on the issue. We call this the Three Chairs Exercise.

Let's say that your coachee, Dawn, identifies that Jordan is causing her tremendous difficulties with a specific task. She has tried everything to manage Jordan and yet it does not seem to make a positive difference. Dawn comes to ask you what she should do. Contracting is an important first step:

I. Explain that you are going to try a coaching technique with her. Agree how much time you have and find a confidential space where you will not be interrupted nor watched. Explain what you are going to do. ▶

II.   Place three chairs in the room next to each other. Agree that one represents Dawn (1st position), one Jordan (2nd position) and the other is for you.

III. Ask Dawn to 'be Dawn'. To sit in Dawn's chair and describe the key issues from her own perspective, taking care to refer to Jordan as if he is present in his chair, pointing and indicating to him. You can encourage Dawn to do this by doing so yourself, 'So what I hear you say Dawn is that Jordan [point to him] refuses to do XYZ and that he [look and nod towards Jordan's chair] says . . . '

IV.   Now ask Dawn to 'be Jordan'. Ask her to move to Jordan's chair and imagine that she is Jordan. Stand as Jordan does. Sit as Jordan does, even speak as he does. Ask Dawn to answer in the first person as if she is Jordan and ask her about the situation. You might try:

   a. So Jordan, you've just heard Dawn describe this situation. What are the most important things you heard?

   b. And Jordan, what do you want Dawn to understand that you think she doesn't get?

   c. Jordan, if you were in Dawn's shoes, how would you move forward on this?

V.   Take care to help Dawn stay in character as Jordan: 'My view is' or 'What I think Dawn should do is . . . '

VI.   When you think Jordan has finished (Jordan, have you said everything you want to say about this?), ask Dawn to come back to 'be Dawn', move back to her chair, take a moment to literally shake her body and shake off Jordan. Now ask Dawn to share her thinking.

You may find it helpful to move to 3rd position as well. You both stand away from the two chairs, looking directly at them, and you might ask (remembering that she is not being Dawn at the moment), 'So. We've just heard a discussion of the issues between Dawn and Jordan. As an independent observer, what have you heard? What would you recommend?'

This technique can be immensely powerful. We have both seen people in tears over seemingly simple work tasks as they understand the reality of the other person's perspective. Phil once coached a volunteer this way in front of a group of leaders learning coaching skills and having been in 1st position for five minutes, moved to 2nd position and immediately burst into tears. After a few moments regaining composure she moved back to her own chair (1st position) and said, 'I'm sorry. I know what to do now. I've seen it. We don't need to continue.'

Look for an opportunity to practise this technique and be aware that it will stretch many of your other coaching skills too, such as the ability to listen and ask great questions. Be clear with your coachee that you are also experimenting. And relax, allowing time for this reflective work.

3. An alternative approach on gaining different perspectives is to ask your coachee to imagine that they have succeeded in reaching the goal they aspire to. And then explore how things look from that perspective:

- How do you feel now?
- What barriers did you overcome to reach here?
- What resources did you need?
- Who helped you?

From here your coachee can identify how they can achieve the change they desire in the way they desire.

THINGS TO DO BEFORE THE NEXT FLIGHT

Read De Bono, E., 2010. *Lateral thinking: a textbook of creativity*. Penguin UK. This book is full of great ideas and includes a version of the perceptual perspectives exercise.

Read Nancy Kline's '*Time to Think: Listening to Ignite the Human Mind*', published in 1999 by Hachette UK.

You can watch several examples of Nancy Kline's ideas on YouTube. We provide links via our website.

For further resources go to: www.coachingonthego.co.uk

Chapter 8

Understanding through empathy: maintaining your altitude

How to listen in a way that generates action

Many leaders we work with roll their eyes when we teach listening skills. The irony is that when we ask for a demonstration of good listening, these are the very people who consistently fail to listen beyond the basic every-day version of listening – they consistently miss points and project their own point of view. If you are rolling your eyes now – well, enough said.

Research has consistently shown that the ability to listen is a key part of leadership and high listening competence improves decision-making. Makes sense, right? Listening well means that you will absorb information better. A survey sent to hundreds of companies in the United States found that poor listening skills create problems at all levels because it creates misunderstandings and re-work. But while we advocate a particular style of listening in coaching situations, in general, leaders and executives will benefit from being versatile in terms of listening type and style in order to adapt to the diverse listening needs of employees, clients/customers, colleagues and other stakeholders.

Within a coaching context, the skill of listening is so important that it is directly identified by several of the main coaching professional bodies as a specific competency that coaches have to demonstrate to gain accreditation (see Part 3: The Pilot's manual). Indeed, some leadership development consultancies base their entire methodology around the impact of skilful listening.

Listening plays a central role in establishing and maintaining the relationships we need to foster as leaders. Listening allows us to engage in the self-disclosure process, which is essential for the establishment of trusting working relationships. Disclosure is often mutual with people getting to know each other by sharing increasingly personal information. As a coach, we use listening to encourage disclosure and to provide a psychological reward, through the simple act of recognition. It helps maintain our relationships.

Listening to others and being listened to in return is part of the give-and-take of any interpersonal relationship. Our thoughts and experiences 'back up' inside us and getting them out helps us maintain a positive balance. So, something as routine and seemingly pointless as listening to our romantic partner debrief the events of their day, or a friend retell their weekend adventures, shows that we are taking an interest in their lives and are willing to put our own concerns aside for a moment to attend to their needs. Listening also closely ties to conflict, as a lack of listening often plays a large role in creating conflict, while effective listening helps us resolve it.

When you are listening as a coach, you will be most effective when you can listen from your coachee's perspective. In other words, you are seeking to empathise so fully with your coachee that you understand why they are saying what they are saying. You can sense what is hidden between the words and sentences – what is not said. You can sense and feel the emotions underneath the words. Is your coachee energised or threatened? Is she intrigued or bored? Your role is to enable your coachee to share their deepest thoughts and to find their best way forward. Listening effectively, known as 'generative listening' is critical to this.

Why is **generative listening** so important? Words can often disguise reality. Consciously and unconsciously. So often we use broad descriptions of a situation rather than specific observations. For example, you might say your boss doesn't respect you when in fact what you mean is they're often late for meetings. Generative listening gets behind the words. Both the listener and the speaker learn more about the speaker's real intentions. It sets aside judgements, criticisms, diagnoses of what's wrong and interpretations. It is called generative listening because its aim is to generate new understanding and from that understanding, generate a way forward. Skilful generative listening leads to skilful action because it naturally identifies what's needed. Here is our summary of what it is:

- It's transformational.

- It's expansive, inclusive, global and oriented to the whole system.

- You listen at 360 degrees as though you and the speaker were at the centre of the universe receiving information from everywhere at once.

- All senses are in use in addition to your intuition.

- By 'listening' to what is happening in you, physically and emotionally, you pick up things that may be subconscious for the speaker.

- Your internal chatter has largely been stilled.

- The other person experiences rapt (but not intrusive) attention, has a sense of having been truly seen, and feels known by you – accepted, affirmed and appreciated.

This type of listening relies on many of the skills we've discussed already: the ability to hold a Pause-Point™, powerful questions, personal presence. Mostly, it is an attitude of deep respect for the person talking and an acknowledgement that their experience of life is valid and worthy of consideration.

In the context of coaching as a leader, generative listening will assist you to help your coachee identify what matters most. And to think deeply. Given that coaching is about helping people to find their own solutions to their own questions and to take the greatest ownership of their actions, thinking deeply in this way allows them to search for what they already know, what they can do and how they might apply this to their challenges. And as a boss, this is exactly what you want too – to empower your team to maximise their impact.

You may find it useful to think of a journalist interviewing someone. Journalists are often listening to identify a scoop, something new and newsworthy. So they interrupt and challenge. They seek to surprise their interviewee with an unexpected question that results in the exposure of something salacious. These journalists are not listening generatively. Rather they are listening with a specific intent in mind and as a result many interviewees report the feeling that they were not listened to. And interviewees are trained to get their own point across whatever the interviewer asks – precisely because they know they might not be listened to.

Research also tells us that we all have an inner voice (or voices) we hear at different times. When we tune in to our inner voice while we are trying to listen to someone else it will likely diminish our capabilities as an effective listener. Learning to diminish the impact of this voice will increase your effectiveness when coaching. The technique that most coaches use is called **bracketing** and we show you how to practise this in *Flying Straight and Level* below.

You may find it helpful to consider listening in terms of its different levels. This relates to different styles of listening and its effectiveness from the perspective of a coaching approach. We think it is most useful to think of three levels of listening where the deepest third level is considered generative listening.

Generative listening: Our meaning - understanding through empathy. Listening with your whole body.

Active listening: Their meaning - listening to and between the words.

Passive listening: My meaning - my reaction to the words.

Passive listening

This is the listening we do most of the time, most days – the listening from your own perspective. 'What does this mean for me? How does this affect me?' In the world of business, we regularly attend meetings in order to represent our department or function. This pushes us to listen from a Level 1 perspective.

From a coaching perspective, passive or Level 1 listening is lazy listening and can distort what you hear because you only receive the message through your personal filter. And yet, if you could listen from a deeper level you have the potential to hear and understand so much more. You have the potential to help the speaker share more.

Active listening

This is probably where most business people like to think they operate. Often leaders have been taught to listen attentively to what matters to the other person. Quietening their inner voice by bracketing or setting aside intrusive thoughts and mustering their full concentration on hearing the words as they have meaning to the other person. Noticing, perhaps, that they use an unexpected word or an unusual word to describe something. Noticing too what is not said.

Generative listening

This is a process of absorption where you let go of your ego fully to allow the experience of your coachee to become real to you. When you let go, there is no judging or evaluation, there is simple pure understanding. People who regularly listen in a generative mode say that it takes full presence in body and mind, and there is nothing else that is important to them other than the person who is speaking. You listen with all your faculties – absorbed into the speaker's world view.

Coaching listening is fully generative. This is where we aim to be as coaches, acknowledging that it is difficult to stay here. You're listening beyond just the words and noticing the feelings and emotions beneath. It involves listening with your ears, eyes and intuition. The listener is aiming for maximum empathy and understanding. Seeking to understand why your coachee says what they do.

Tomacz is clearing away the breakfast service in first class. With his natural charm, good looks and attentive ear all the ladies are melting. Men too are in thrall to him. Tomacz has no problem remembering names, menu preferences and personal details. As he picks up the trays, he takes time to show that everyone is

special to him. Even at this other-worldly time everyone is enjoying the moment. It is into this halcyon scene that Caroline steps.

SCENE 8: WAKING UP

Once again, her mood has slipped. If cramped in-flight beds have a wrong side, she has got out on it. Breakfast is late she thinks as she tries to grab the attention of Tomacz. She can't hang around waiting while he schmoozes passengers. She needs to relieve Prya in the cockpit.

Caroline plonks herself in a galley seat and waits for Tomacz to notice her.

'Breakfast?' Caroline injects some sarcasm into her request. Because it's not a request. 'As you wish,' responds Tomacz with equal amounts of sarcasm. He will do it, unwillingly.

Although it only takes five minutes, Caroline can't help showing her impatience. When it does arrive, breakfast is brought to her by Kristoff, another tall, good-looking, perennially smiling crew member. Keeping the breakfast tray out of her grasp, Kristoff leans down, and in a low but unmistakably determined voice, he says: 'Caroline, there's a spare seat at 40J. I'll bring your tray there. The couple in the seats next to you have just got married, they'd be chuffed to meet the first officer. Go do some PR for us. See what you can learn about them? You might also come to appreciate that luxury seat you get at the front of the plane when you suffer 16 inches of leg room.'

It's a verbal slap in the face.

A reluctant Caroline paints on her best smile and walks to the back of the plane. The empty seat is cluttered with debris and politely she moves it aside and slides in to introduce herself. Right on cue, Kristoff arrives with her breakfast. As promised, it is cramped but the passengers are flattered to meet her. She, in turn, finds it is the most natural thing in the world to ask about their wedding and share their joy in going on honeymoon. She settles in and listens to their plans.

Maybe it was the food. Maybe it was the increased levels of blood sugar and good company. As Caroline munches a surprisingly good breakfast, she finds that Kristoff's words have lost their sting.

▶

UsFlyHiPo is fanatical about its passengers. The company lives and breathes customer service and expects everyone to play their part. Without even really noticing, Caroline finds that it is effortless to listen to the couple's chatter. Such a happy time in their life and their fun is infectious – and of course they're on a high having had the first officer listen so attentively to all their plans.

Breakfast over, Caroline positively skips to the galley to find Tomacz. It feels good to apologise and shake hands. It is actually easier to say sorry than keep her nose in the air. She makes a point too of thanking Kristoff for sending her to the back of the plane. She even gives him a kiss on the cheek (to his delight). She'd learnt something about passengers and about herself. That really was special.

Your turn at the controls

Generative listening can be effortless and below we provide some ideas to help you build this skillset. Of itself, the skill of listening is necessary but insufficient to achieve true generative listening. The main pre-requisite of generative listening is a particular set of beliefs about coaching.

The first belief is that when coaching it is *their* learning and *their* work. This was most powerfully illustrated to Jenny when she was training during an exercise where she did nothing but listen fully, intently and with her whole self. In that exercise, the coachee miraculously talked themselves to a satisfactory conclusion. Jenny did nothing, she was merely a conduit for the coachee. Except of course, this is *everything*. Just the act of being there and witnessing another person talk through their situation is an act of generosity. Fully being there gives permission, space and safety for the coachee to do their work.

The second belief is that you may be older, wiser, smarter or more senior than your coachee, but you are definitely not there to fix them or their situation. To embody this belief is to let go, relax, allow, and mostly it is to trust. The trust you hold is that the process will work and it doesn't require your intervention nor your brainpower. In trusting that listening is the gift you give, you can let go of your ego and become the conduit for your coachee to think out loud.

In short, to be a generative listener, your work as a coach is to show up fully and to trust.

 ## FLYING STRAIGHT AND LEVEL

1. For the next week, become aware of your judgements when you are listening. Watch when you are compelled to jump in, interrupt and express an opinion. Notice and record how much you interrupt people compared to others.

2. Whichever level of listening you are practising, as a listener you should not steal the spotlight from the speaker. Offer support without offering your own story or advice. In meetings watch who has the spotlight . . . and who steals it. Watch yourself too and note if you take the spotlight when you were trying to listen. Look for patterns. Do you do this more with certain people? Or on certain topics? What impact does this have on the outcomes?

3. For the next week, each time you enter into a conversation of any type, before you join (or as you join if you had no warning) ask yourself what purpose you have in listening to this. It could be any of the following:

   • To empathise and build trust or respect.

   • To motivate a co-worker.

   • To identify gaps or weaknesses to improve your negotiation position.

   • To understand.

   • To gather data to be able to represent your team or department's perspective.

▶

- To relax.
- To learn.

   This process will help to clarify how you want to listen and whether generative listening is appropriate. It is clearly not always appropriate and different listening approaches may be better in different listening contexts.

4. Once you have found your sloppy listening habits, make a commitment to nourish some good listening habits. Start by 'bracketing' intrusive thoughts:

   - Bracketing means that you keep your attention on the person talking and you are not distracted by your own priorities.

   - By using bracketing you can systematically put aside thoughts that are getting in the way of your listening.

   - Every time you are listening, notice when you hear your inner voice with an independent thought speaking. For example, it might say, 'I wonder what the time is?' or 'I promised to do that report by the end of today'. When this happens, say to yourself, 'I will come back to that later', or 'For now, I can park my thoughts.' With practice you will notice this allows you to focus quickly back on the speaker.

 LOOPING THE LOOP

1. For this exercise you will need a buddy to practise with. Do not take notes but try to become fully immersed in the experience of listening and have the confidence that you will remember what was said. Take turns trying the following for ten minutes each:

   - The speaker talks about an aspect of their work that they have been thinking about recently.

   - The listener just gives full attention and allows the speaker to explore their thoughts and feelings and desire for action.

   - The listener seeks to pick up what the speaker is:

      o **Thinking**: What is being said, the pattern of thoughts. Is it logical, detailed or general? In the past, present or future? Who is being talked about and who is not? What images and metaphors are being used? What assumptions are being made?

- **Feeling**: What is the speaker feeling? Notice the gestures, posture, tone of voice, way of breathing, the expression of the face and eye movement.

- **Willing**: What does the speaker want to do? What is just a wish and what is a definite intention to act?

  At the end of the ten minutes, the listener starts by playing back their observations under the three headings. The speaker responds with a reflection on what it feels like to be heard like this. Swap roles and repeat.

2. Take the experience of this exercise and try to reach the same egoless state in another conversation. A normal conversation. A conversation where you have not declared this generative listening intention. Do not take notes. Again, have confidence that fully absorbed listening will be enough for you to remember what is really important.

- Reflect on what happens . . .

- . . . and repeat

THINGS TO DO BEFORE THE NEXT FLIGHT

Read Nancy Kline's *'Time to think: Listening to Ignite the Human Mind'*, published in 1999 by Hachette UK.

You can watch several examples of Nancy Kline's ideas on YouTube.

Read Douglas Stone, Sheila Heen and Bruce Patton *'Difficult Conversations: How to Discuss What Matters'*. It's the basis of a course at Harvard University on negotiation.

Read Stephen Covey's *'The 7 Habits of Highly Effective People: Powerful Lessons in Personal Change'*, published in 1989 by Simon Schuster UK

Read Marshall B Rosenberg's *'Nonviolent Communication: A Language of Life'*.

Watch Celeste Headlee's 'How to Have a Good Conversation' on TEDxCreativeCoast, 2015: we provide a link on our website.

Watch William Ury's 'The Power of Listening' on TEDxSanDiego, 2015: the link can be found via our website.

Listen to our podcast, sponsored by Cranfield University where you will hear Sandra Krisberger-Sinigoi talk about the power of questions.

For further resources go to: www.coachingonthego.co.uk

Chapter 9

Succeeding together: onward and upward

Using delegation as learning opportunities

Jenny vividly remembers when she first became managing director of a company and how quickly she was overwhelmed by the job and the number of people who came into her office each day with problems that they expected her to solve. No matter how many hours she worked, she could never get on top of the workload. Her problem was that she hadn't learnt how to successfully delegate (and it's now a particular coaching speciality).

Note that the operative word is 'successfully' delegate and that's what we will explore here. Most of us know how to ask others in our team to take on a task, but many of us fail to set them up for success.

We need to stress that the skill of delegation is not generally considered to be a skill of an effective coach. The coaching professional bodies do not identify delegation as a skill of coaching – and this is completely logical because if a coach delegated their responsibilities to the coachee, then what would the coach do? And yet there is a clear overlap between effective coaching and effective delegation. The key skills in coaching overlap with the key skills of delegating, such as contracting, listening, questioning and building rapport. Given that we regularly work with leaders who want to delegate more effectively, adding this skill seems not just sensible but a great way to build your coaching capabilities at the same time.

The recurring problem that we see when we coach leaders is that they complain that those they delegate to fail to deliver to their standards or meet deadlines, or don't fully understand what's needed or come up with superficial answers. Never was there a clearer need for coaching skills.

We have seen two very distinct mindsets around the issue of delegating. The first is flavoured with a hint of guilt. That is, a leader who feels slightly guilty at asking someone else to take on a task. Their assumption is that if they had time, they would do it themselves and therefore delegation can be seen as dumping unwanted tasks on to someone else. When we have this attitude, we take shortcuts in setting up the situation, we often don't brief the other person well, we don't share all the needed information – we ping a quick email to the other person and leave them to it. Not surprisingly, they don't do a good job. In fact, they can't do a good job and when this situation prevails it sets up a downward cycle.

Belief that delegation is dumping

Don't set the person up to succeed

Sub-standard result

Confirms a view that others can't do this as well as you

Take on too much work

Overwork/exhaustion

Delegation downward spiral

By contrast, a second mindset flips this attitude completely the other way and considers delegation as an opportunity to provide someone else with an assignment where they can grow and develop. Leaders who hold this mindset think carefully about offering other people the chance to take on assignments that will truly stretch them. These leaders use their coaching skills to continually support someone who is trying to complete a challenging project. They invest a significant amount of time briefing them carefully so they have access to the necessary information, resources and people.

Rather than expecting to be disappointed by the delivery of their team member, they fully expect the best, but they also know that they continue to have full accountability for supporting that person throughout. Quite simply, we can only imagine a very few roles where it is possible to delegate without engaging the coaching mode.

Effective delegation generates a win–win. It enables the leader (coach) to be more effective and it enables the team member (coachee) to be more effective while acknowledging this is an important part of the contracting process. This is especially true in matrixed organisations when several different leaders may be delegating work to the same people. Partnerships, such as management consulting firms, are good examples of this environment. It's important to build a strong rapport with your coachees as leaders are effectively competing for the same resource.

There are three patches of air turbulence to fly through. The first, and often most pre-eminent, is that coachees must be allowed to do the delegated tasks their way as much as is possible – not your way. When delegating, let them know if there are deadlines and requirements to report upwards. Or any other constraints. The coaching element is to help them figure out how they will achieve success in the assignment. Which means, and here's the second air pocket. . .

. . . at some point, something will go wrong. Your coachee is learning. This exposes them to making mistakes. From failing to update you as you agreed, to failing to deliver as expected. Effective delegation provides safety blankets (and flotation devices) to limit the possibility of failure and protect the project. Any leader who delegates must be prepared for this possibility to allow their coachee to be fully stretched. The upside, remember, is that you have saved a considerable amount of your time, which will increase as your coachee's abilities increase. Hence, overall you win.

The other bit of air turbulence is that sometimes a leader has to delegate boring work. Work that the coachee is no longer learning from, except perhaps at the margins. You need to contract for this. This is correct organisational management – the boss's time costs the firm more and should be dedicated to the more complex or remunerative tasks. It's part of the deal.

And you still need to make sure that the balance of your coachee's work remains interesting and motivational.

In contracting with your team member around the more mundane work, you can use your coaching skills to think of interesting ways for them to work so that although the task is boring the completion is not. Examples are working with others in new ways to collect data or presenting some learning back to the team.

What to delegate?

So, how do you decide what assignments to complete yourself, which assignments to delegate, and how do you set up others for success?

There's a wonderful piece of organisation theory by Elliott Jaques (it's quite old, but we believe still relevant) that says that each layer of an organisation should take on qualitatively different levels of work. This means that the assignments you take on at your level should tackle different strategic or operational problems to those of your team. Equally, your boss should be tackling the next level of problems. The best and most efficient organisations have little overlap between these layers. If you have too much overlap this feels like micro management, whereas if you have no overlap, issues and concerns don't get resolved and get pushed around the structure with no resolution.

Here's a partial, and fictitious, example taken from UsFlyHiPo:

- Level 1, The Board: Looking at mergers and acquisitions with competitors, considering new business opportunities, expansion or consolidation. Considering the regulatory environment and future major shifts that might pose an existential threat. Set the strategy according to their consolidated view of the next five to ten years.

- Level 2, The Senior Leadership Team: Looking at travel trends and technological innovations, what routes should the airline fly, which planes to buy. Major decisions, within the strategy.

- Level 3, The Leadership Team: Looking across policies and procedures to bring the strategy into reality. How do all the moving parts of the business need to interconnect. How to optimise current resources.

- Level 4, First Level Leadership: Looking down single or several policies and procedures to ensure they are coherent and cohesive.

- Level 5, Operations: Etc.:

When we are feeling uncertain of ourselves it is easy to creep down to the level below where your organisation wants you to operate. This is because these are the tasks we can accomplish easily and so they help us build our confidence and sense of achievement. But this is false security because it has an impact on our team by robbing them of learning opportunities. It keeps us busy but it keeps us from being more strategic or taking the bigger picture.

A simple way to consider whether you are working at the right level in relation to your team is to think about the time horizon of the issues and problems you deal with. For example, if you're regularly thinking about things that will be important for the company in a year – so you are generally looking ahead 12 months – then we expect your boss is looking beyond that time horizon. Equally, your team should be working up to that time horizon. Another very simple example would be where your team undertake similar tasks and your role is primarily to coordinate their activity to ensure new tasks can be accommodated all the time. Each team member works on a single task in the present and your role is to make sure someone is available for the next task.

What you absolutely want to make sure of is that you are not solving problems that your team should be working on. You have extra in your pay cheque, because you are working that extra time horizon ahead. Be firm with yourself about the problems you can *uniquely* solve and whether that's appropriate to your role. Then make sure that you're not creeping down a level to do easier tasks.

As you will have come to expect, Prya has the mindset that delegation is all about empowerment and development. She has full confidence in Caroline. Prya has such confidence she will even put herself and a plane load of people at risk.

For the final hours of the long trip, Caroline relieves Prya of command to even out the workload.

Today their destination is a famously beautiful location surrounded by snowy mountains, with a scary reputation among Pilots for its narrow approach to the runway. The flight has been long but Caroline has enjoyed it. Prya had previously suggested that Caroline handle the landing. Caroline is confident that her first time at the legendry Granite Peaks will go smoothly, she has rehearsed it many times in the simulator and she's reviewed the flight plan. It is so typical of those macho Pilots to talk up the steep gorge and waterfalls apparently coming out of the clouds. To boast of the difficulty of coping with mountain flying and low cloud. But Caroline has looked at the landing plates often enough to be sure she can cope.

SCENE 9: THE LANDING

But here it is, Granite Peaks, and Caroline is sweating – the reality is nothing like the simulator training. The vector to the landing system requires a 10 degree turn to the right and all she can see, just off the wing tip, is the famous granite wall. Suddenly the Istanbul incident demands Caroline's attention.

'Oh no, not another failure.' She thinks. 'She can't mess this one up. Prya is a snitch and will tell FC if things go wrong.'

Caroline turns to look at the granite mountain. All is not well. She freezes in horror at the prospect of turning the plane towards it. She wills the plane into submission but the facts don't change. She is off course. Meanwhile, Prya is calling the numbers. Her voice hasn't changed a note. There is no sign of panic or reprimand here. There is no sign of doubt.

▶

But the runway is not on the nose. Caroline needs to make that turn towards the mountain and time and space are running out. With adrenaline high, and the banging of her heart sounding in her ears, Caroline turns to Prya, who simply indicates right and smiles reassuringly. In that instant, Caroline and Prya know, there is no hiding her fear. This is no place for bravado.

'I always find this a tough one,' says Prya encouragingly,

'Yeah' chimes Asif from behind. 'Looks great on paper, but not a favourite place of mine either.'

Prya chuckles, 'I remember the first time you flew with us here Asif. You were almost as white as the snow out there!'

Prya continues, 'Follow the plates Caroline, you can do it.'

Caroline feels herself smiling and she notices her shoulders relax. She breathes a bit deeper and her shoulders relax a bit more. In the end, the course correction was effortless, and the remainder of the landing was on the numbers. Air traffic control even greeted her with a 'G'day'. Caroline smiled.

As Prya took over for the taxi to the gate, Caroline feels the tension ebb away and a wave of relief wash over her. Mostly, she is grateful that Prya has been so gracious about it all. There was no gloating or commentary on her loss of nerve. There was not even a suggestion that this would go down in her personal log as a 'development opportunity'. What on earth did that mean anyway? Prya had taken it all in her stride.

Caroline thinks, 'I needed help and finally I was more scared of missing the mark than admitting I needed support. How silly am I? Of course, I don't know it all and I need help sometimes. Flying these big beasts is a team game.'

It feels like a milestone and she looks forward to sleeping well that night.

Your turn at the controls

Notice the soft words of encouragement and support that Prya provides when delegating. She has given Caroline the opportunity and advance notice and remains ready to help – without taking over.

These next activities focus on improving your delegation skills and the coaching skills that make delegation successful. In so doing, you will build a more effective team and you will be a more effective leader.

 FLYING STRAIGHT AND LEVEL

1. Identify the differentiating factors between your role and that of your team members following the organisational level model described above. Review your activities and check that they are consistent with this model. Any inconsistencies need delegating downwards (or possibly upwards).

2. Identify how much work you delegate versus how much you want to delegate. Set yourself targets to increase. While this alone will not change the effectiveness of how you delegate, it will create a focus of attention on the issue that these further actions will help you to achieve.

3. Review with each person in your team their development and start a conversation about what assignments they have seen others take on in the past that they would have liked. Agree with them the type of projects, tasks and problems that they would like to be assigned in the future so that they can be stretched and learn new things.

4. Once a day for the next month, ask one person in your team: 'How can I support you on xyz?' or 'What would be most helpful to you on abc?' or 'Is there information or contacts or experience that I have that you need to help you succeed at . . . ?' (See also Part 3: The Pilot's manual, on weekly one-to-one meetings.)

5. Set up a team meeting where you draw out the levels of the organisation and jointly agree the time horizon that you operate on and identify the one for the team. Expect this to be a bit uncomfortable and use all ▶

your coaching skills to really listen – most of us learn some truths in these discussions as we're not as good at delegating as we would like to be. Now ask everyone to check that they are operating at the right level.

6. Set up a one-to-one discussion with each team member to clarify how you are currently delegating, how you would like to delegate and hence what's changing. Seek their feedback.

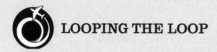 **LOOPING THE LOOP**

1. Set up a one-to-one meeting with someone where their role description is the basis of the conversation. Have their role description ready for the meeting and look at it together. Ask them what they uniquely do at this level. Check with them whether they are clear on their contribution and how they fit into the larger structure of the organisation.

2. Be brave and delegate an assignment to someone in your team that you know will really stretch them. Invest time and energy in setting them up for success. Give them a buddy in the team who can act as a mentor. Check in with them regularly and offer to listen to their problems and issues. Bring out your best coaching to help *them* to problem-solve. Do not take the assignment back and complete it yourself. And do not let them fail. Then spend some time reflecting.

3. Hold after-action-reviews for your team and for subsets of your team. Use appreciative inquiry to gather the learning (See Chapter 5).

4. Run pre-mortems with individuals and your team. A pre-mortem is *before* things go wrong, and an opportunity to ask what might go wrong and how to prevent it. The pre-mortem operates on the assumption that the project has failed, and so asks what did go wrong. Although both questions invite your coachee to imagine, it seems that asking people to mentally stand in a future and look back is an easier cognitive task and generates more useful ideas. You simply ask them to generate plausible reasons for this failure. This way of encouraging discussion about failure is powerful because it circumvents someone's anxiety about being politically correct.

5. Celebrate success loudly and publicly, making others into heroes.

THINGS TO DO BEFORE THE
NEXT FLIGHT

Read Elliott Jaques' ideas on work levels in the *Harvard Business Review:* we provide a link on our website

For further resources go to: www.coachingonthego.co.uk

Chapter **10**

Creating actions to move forward: smooth landings

Developing meaningful follow-up

All the good insight that coaching can create is nothing if it's not backed up by action. Action generates change. Actual people doing things, and possibly doing them differently. Or indeed people no longer doing things. Actions can be as simple as thinking about something in more detail or reflecting further. And like many elements of coaching it may sound straightforward, but there is still a great skill in helping your coachee identify their actions. The criticality is that, in line with the principle that the coachee is responsible and accountable for their actions, they need to be actions that the coachee believes will move them forward. They need to be motivational. So, at what point and how, during a coaching conversation, do you move to action?

Your listening skills are fundamental to this capability. You are listening for the possibility of ideas and actions. Sometimes you may hear your coachee ponder out loud, 'I wonder if I should ask some of my colleagues for their ideas and how they do it?' This could be an opportunity. And you also need to listen to their emotions. Do they sound positive about this idea or does it sound overwhelming? If it sounds positive you might suggest they should act upon it. Alternatively, if it sounds like a big challenge you may need to help them explore further, 'How useful do you think it might be to ask some of your colleagues for their ideas?' Or even more simply, you might ask, 'Your colleagues?' Notice this uses the skill of summarising. What you are listening for here is their energy.

Energy levels are really important to effective coaching. Your skills at generative listening will enable both you and your coachee to notice when their energy is positive and enabling. Your skills at questioning will help move them towards that energy. When you hear it, it's an invitation to move towards an action. These points can happen at any time. They need not be at the end of a conversation, so don't wait. Take action (as the coach) to help your coachee find actions. Of course, subsequent thinking might generate a change to an earlier action. No problem. Make the change. Make a new action.

While you will have conversations where your coachee keeps putting fuel into the engine of actions, sometimes necessitating an action of prioritising, other times you may not have heard any potential actions and time is drawing to a close. In which case the coach needs to take action.

Remember the behavioural experiment idea as this is a perfect way to agree a way forward (in Part 1 we devote a whole section to behavioural experiments, if you need a refresher). We often spend time in a coaching conversation working with our coachees to design behavioural experiments that will give them the opportunity to try something new and reflect on how it turns out.

If creating behavioural experiments feels too elaborate for you, remember Anja who simply asked: 'And when might you do that?' Whichever way you choose to do it, the aim is for the coaching conversation to conclude with simple next steps and an agreement about what's expected. In keeping with the principle that they do the work, it is likely that most of the actions will be theirs, but one or two might rely on you contributing too. And always complete the exercise by agreeing when you will talk again to check in on progress and see what further support you can offer. This does not mean you cannot discuss it before then if the coachee wants to. Rather, it creates a supportive backstop position.

Should you seem to be in the joyous position where your coachee has identified lots of actions, you need to check in with them (a form of contracting) regarding the practicality and realism of such a list. Could they look at the list tomorrow and feel daunted by it? Are they setting themselves up for failure? A good way to help check in here is to use the famous SMART acronym for setting goals.

In our experience, reference to the SMART acronym generates a range of responses from the positive to the outright despondent, such as 'We always go on about SMART until I lose the will to carry on.' In leadership and coaching workshops with multinational participants we consistently find over half the delegates are not familiar with it. So our advice is never assume someone has heard of it.

There are variations of the SMART acronym so feel free to check out alternatives. It was created by George Doran, although sadly for him it's such a good mnemonic acronym that no one remembers him. His paper, based on motivational theories, stated that objectives should be:

Specific   – target a specific area for improvement.

Measurable   – quantify or at least suggest an indicator of progress.

Assignable   – specify who will do it.

Realistic   – state what results can realistically be achieved, given available resources.

Time-related – specify when the result(s) can be achieved.

You can use SMART by asking your coachee to apply it to each of their actions. So taking the earlier example: What do they intend to learn from their colleagues? How many colleagues could be asked? How many is it realistic to ask? Are there some that it might be inappropriate (unrealistic) to ask? By when will you ask them?

You may also find that these questions generate further thinking on the original action. For example, on the action's specificity, asking how that will help can easily lead to further valuable thinking.

Think carefully as a coach about when to gain this clarity for each action. If your generative listening and powerful questioning has raised the energy and your coachee is thinking of lots of actions, you might suggest they note each action down first while the energy remains high and then come back to their notes to improve and strengthen their potential.

Creating an action plan is also a great time to think about using summarising and paraphrasing as a way to wrap up a conversation while checking in on the impact of the actions. 'So, to gain feedback on how effective you are in client meetings, you're going to talk to five peers in your department within the next fortnight. Is that correct?'

Phil likes to use a specific final step, which he offers at the end of most coaching conversations. He asks if it would be useful to the coachee if they were to write out all their actions in a short email and send it to him after the conversation. He explains that the reason people like to do this is that it requires a little further reflection and some accuracy in the wording, which continues to help the coachee focus on what they want. It also increases their sense of accountability and responsibility, although Phil does not point that out. Finally, it gives the coachee a clear reference point to move forward, which can be used to discuss progress next time with Phil. In a work conversation you may not need to use that email again. It just helps your coachee. And, as you would expect, it remains confidential.

What happens if no progress is made?

Sometimes you may find that having agreed a set of actions, the next time you speak to each other it becomes clear that no progress has been made. That few or none of the actions have been followed up. What do you do?

Remember that coaching is focused on moving forward and finding new ways to address challenges. It is often not helpful, nor consistent with the coaching ethos, to focus on what prevented progress. The coaching skill here is to look for the positives and steps that can be built on. At its simplest, a coachee might say that after further reflection they no longer felt that these actions were appropriate. The positive step to acknowledge is that they have spent further time reflecting on their circumstances. And the implication is that there is still something that is affecting the coachee's progress that had not surfaced previously. Engage your coaching skills once again to help them think about and explore their thinking, to identify what might be in the way and find a new way forward. This might be something completely new, just one of the previous actions or the same actions now with a greater sense of purpose.

Turning back to our story, Caroline is clearly feeling and acting less like a victim, and she seems to jump into new situations with some alacrity, all to good effect.

So now we are all trying to get off the plane first, jumping up even though the seat belt light is still on. Sitting back down grumbling that it was someone else's fault when chastised by the crew. We've all been there.

The airport is small and there are not many passport booths open (are they on strike again?) and everyone is nervous that they filled out the wrong form or will stand in the wrong queue.

▶

SCENE 10: ENDLESS QUEUES

Little did Caroline and the crew know what would await them. The airport terminal is rammed. The holiday crowds are arriving by the plane load, and clearly the airport is at capacity. Chaos. Kids crying with fatigue, the air con struggling to bring the temperature to bearable level. And endless queues. It is clear their passengers are facing possibly an hour or more of shuffling forward to immigration.

Normally, Caroline couldn't care less. Her job was done – she'd got them safely to their destination – and, by way of reward, her and the crew have a special fast-track channel. Like greyhounds the crew head for the exit and their hotel bus.

Not so fast, thinks Caroline. Isn't this part of the travel experience? Why do we assume our job is done?

The fluorescent orange boarding passes that UsFlyHiPo passengers hold in their hand clearly identify where her customers stand in the queue and the legions of people ahead. Quite spontaneously, Caroline begins to work her way down the line. Stopping occasionally to talk to people, reassuring everyone they're in the right line, occasionally checking their paperwork, which confuses even sane people let alone those with 17 hours of jetlag. Inside she can feel the urge to hurry, to rush for that inviting bus that is waiting outside. But she resists and patiently keeps walking down the queues.

In fact, the little help she gives is invaluable. Everyone notices and is appreciative. No one begrudges her the fast-track exit. The bus hasn't waited. It's a small setback and Caroline doesn't let it dent her sense of satisfaction. It is the glow of a job well done.

Your turn at the controls

You may have heard that it takes tens of thousands of hours to become expert in something and, while that is a gross generalisation, it does rest on some solid research. What the research actually said was that people who become expert undertake something called 'deliberate practice'. Dr K Anders Ericsson has studied what it takes to get to be the best and, while that may not be exactly what you aim for with your coachees, there are definitely lessons to be learned from his research. Most importantly, deliberate practice requires us to get out of our comfort zone and to deliberately try new things. That is the essence of the tools that we present here.

 FLYING STRAIGHT AND LEVEL

1. When coaching conversations are drawing to a close, use summaries or paraphrasing to check that you can move to a close.

2. In future meetings, ask people to summarise back to the group the actions they will take.

3. In future meetings, always summarise to the group any actions that you agreed to take. Make these as SMART as possible.

4. Next time you notice someone is not suggesting or moving to an action, ask what they will do next and by when.

5. Ask your coachees to use when/then statements to design their actions points: When a customer gets mad with me on the service support desk, then I will start to use the new protocol.

6. Agree when you will check in with your coachee to hear how they are getting on. If you are also their organisational leader, remind them that you are holding them accountable for these actions, which are just as important as other actions they have in their role.

LOOPING THE LOOP

1. Jointly design some behavioural experiments with coachees for them to try out. Experiments need to spell out the new behaviour (and particularly how it differs from the current behaviour), as well as a commitment to note what difference this change produces.

   For example, instead of procrastinating every month over the sales report, I will aim to have a first draft ready by the 3rd of the month and the final draft ready by the 7th of the month. I will notice how my feelings of guilt and incompetence change when I keep to these deadlines.

   Or, I will put time in my diary every month to have a meeting with myself and I will treat that meeting as if I was a customer. In the meeting with myself, I will spend time doing the research/work/thinking that I don't get to do when I rush from meeting to meeting. I will notice how spending this time every month improves my contribution to strategic discussions.

   Make sure you agree when you will check in with your coachee to hear how they are getting on and to offer further support and coaching.

2. Review all the goals and objectives currently set for you and your team members and evaluate whether they meet the SMART criteria. If not, change your own goals accordingly and then take the opportunity to explain to your team how SMART goals work and ask each of them individually to adjust their personal objectives accordingly. Then review the new objectives and discuss any consequences.

3. Repeat the above process with a colleague or peer without necessarily identifying it as a coaching conversation. For example, if you have a task to create a report and you are concerned how to illustrate some of the data most effectively, agree to create three different ways of illustrating this and asking three different colleagues or stakeholders for their views.

THINGS TO DO BEFORE THE
NEXT FLIGHT

Read K A Ericsson, R T Krampe and C Tesch-Römer 'The role of deliberate practice in the acquisition of expert performance' in *Psychological Review*, 100(3), p. 363 (1993).

Read George T Doran's 'There's a S.M.A.R.T. way to write management's goals and objectives' in *Management Review*, AMA FORUM. 70 (11), pp. 35–36 (1981).

Read Caroline Webb's *'How To Have A Good Day'*, *The Essential Toolkit for a Productive Day at Work and Beyond*.

For further resources go to: www.coachingonthego.co.uk

Chapter 11

Learning to learn

Time for reflection

Throughout this book we have included a suggestion to reflect. Here we want to explore what reflection is and why we place so much emphasis on it. It would be easy to take for granted that everyone knows how to reflect, and yet our experience suggests otherwise. Sometimes there's an assumption that reflection simply happens, somehow. Asking your coachee how they reflect on the challenges they face can often generate long silences (and reflection) to find an answer. We encourage you to use reflection when you are coaching and to be explicit about what it means.

Because reflection requires you to stop and take time out of action to review the action, it can feel like an artificial process. We especially notice this in the technology industry where people are working so hard and fast they really struggle to take time out for any reflection.

'Insanity is doing the same thing over and over again and expecting different results'.

Attributed wrongly to Einstein

This has been attributed to various people and organisations over the ages, but there is no definitive proof!
Quite simply, reflection stops you working insanely.

Taking our own advice therefore, let's unpack reflection. Reflection, or reflective practice, is the ability to think through an action (or lack of action) in order to learn from it. This means that it is a conscious effort to identify what went well and what did not go well in order to consider whether future actions might need to change to generate better outcomes.

Reflection requires you and your coachees to examine and experiment with your deeply held assumptions about the world. We encourage you to learn how to do this examination privately through reflection with yourself before you apply it to a coaching situation. The easiest way to do this reflection is to ask why or a variation of why. Let's illustrate this with an example.

I want a promotion – why?

Because I think I deserve it – why?

Because I have been in this job for two years now – why is that a good reason?

Because the company should value my work and reward me for it – why is a promotion the way to do that?

Because it confers status and importance and shows that I'm valued – why is status the way for the company to show you that you're valued?

Because I want the status.

OK. Through this reflection we have found the underlying mental model, or assumption about the world. This understanding can now become the place to start because a particular world view is keeping an underlying world view 'I want a promotion' as a fixed concept. When we reveal a deep assumption such as 'I want status' it allows us to see how this assumption might be in conflict with other assumptions, such as 'status doesn't matter, what really matters is that people have fun at work'.

By the way, you will see in Part 3: The Pilot's manual, that we are cautious about the use of questions that begin with 'why'. People can be very defensive when we ask 'why', yet it is still important to understand what motivates them.

If you want to use this type of reflection with your coachee, you can easily turn why questions into what questions: 'What's behind that?' or 'What belief supports that?' Here is a model that might help you become better at reflection for yourself and with the people you coach.

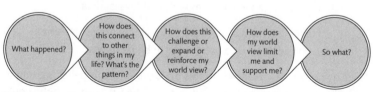

Reflection questions

We've given you a lot of good basic psychological reasons to explain why our world view is very fixed and holds us in tight patterns of behaviour. This applies to pretty much everyone, so don't take it personally. In the spirit of coaching and expanding the behavioural repertoire, reflection is invaluable. Finding the world view, values or assumptions that keep a behaviour in place is the way to begin to achieve sustainable change. Using a very good friend of ours as an example, he might reflect on his lateness and come to discover something new.

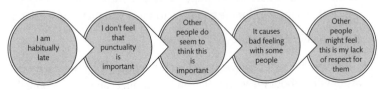

Reflection questions: an example

Reflection can also help you to notice when behaviour is driven by your values or by beliefs about the world. By way of example, here's a recent case from a coaching conversation one of us has had. This coachee had received feedback that they needed to be more strategic and we used a reflection on values to help understand what was driving their current behaviour. (Obviously this was a confidential conversation, so we've taken liberties with the dialogue and also used '. . . .' to indicate that far more was said in the conversation.)

. . . in summary, the feedback is that you are too much in the weeds and you will be more effective when you work more strategically . . . What is your guess about what keeps you in the weeds . . . ?

. . . I love detail and think accuracy is really important . . .

. . . what personal value resonates with that love of detail?

. . . . accuracy is a form of honesty . . . I'm an honest person . . . If things aren't accurate, I can't be sure I'm being honest . . .

Once again, we can really see in this dialogue how this belief is going to keep this person completely fixed and attached to a set of behaviours that the organisation is saying holds them back from being promoted. If we ask them to let go of their attention to detail, we're in danger of asking them to be dishonest – and we can all see that that is going to make them unhappy (rightly so?), and that it is going to be unsustainable behaviour. If you were coaching this individual and you hadn't uncovered this assumption, then the riddle of how to help them work more strategically would have remained unsolved. By making the hidden belief visible, you and the coachee know what they think and why, and you can work on a way forward.

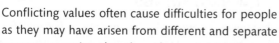

Conflicting values often cause difficulties for people as they may have arisen from different and separate sources, meaning that the values are logical, positive and enabling in their original context and yet have come to create conflict. Furthermore, these values may be subconscious or deeply embedded despite the consequences of the conflict being visible. Another example is personal loyalty to the organisation you work for and doing what's considered right for the organisation versus your own personal beliefs. This might manifest itself in charging a price for a product that you think someone cannot afford. The art of reflection and enabling others to reflect can make this come to the surface. (Various techniques can help you explore coachee's belief systems (often referred to as limiting beliefs). For example the Three Chairs Exercise or the Up, Down and Around™ model.)

Remember from the Welcome on board section that this is their work to do, not yours. You can help – if you are coaching you have a duty to help – but not to fix or solve. In the example above, having found the underlying assumption that accuracy is a form of honesty, you can reflect it back to them (using a summary) and ask them to explore that. You can ask them to reflect on that belief, not to change it, but to understand it and how it is affecting their behaviour.

Caroline doesn't have the benefit of a coach to help her with this type of reflection, but we can tell that she is beginning to examine her deep beliefs and that when they are brought into the light of day, things shift.

It's the day after Caroline's first landing at Granite Peaks. Some of the crew are already outside enjoying the early morning sunshine by the hotel pool – and considering a cocktail. Caroline is resting in the lounge and enjoying the mountainous views.

SCENE 11: NEW BEGINNINGS

Caroline isn't even thinking about work when her phone flashes an incoming call, so she answers unconsciously and with a cursory 'Hello'. The warm voice on the other end introduces himself as Bruce, a headhunter, and Caroline goes from relaxed to alert in an instant.

Of course, she'd been flattered by calls such as this in the past, with their thinly veiled formulaic questions. But this was clearly going to be a different kind of conversation. Bruce cuts right to the chase. He knows she has failed a promotion this week. He guesses she is feeling raw and aggrieved. Why not find a new employer, one that would see her talent and acknowledge her true worth? He knows just the place. An exciting opportunity at JumboJumbo airlines offering a generous package and, more importantly, she'd be guaranteed that promotion.

It was that fast and that easy. The prize. Lying on a plate right in front of her.

But what happened next to Caroline is as unexpected as the conversation with FC that she'd failed to comprehend two days ago. It dawns on her what FC was saying. For the first time, she actually hears and understands the feedback, that promotion is an all-round calibration, not just her flying ability but her leadership too. He's right, she hasn't been showing her ability to find flexible solutions to problems, she leans too much on rank. Nor is she sufficiently concerned with the team's wellbeing, focusing too much on the achievement of her objectives.

Bruce's voice penetrates her reverie. 'Interested to hear your thoughts, Caroline?' he concludes. She opens her mouth to speak, and surprises herself again. 'Well, two days ago I would have bitten your hand off for that promotion, but right now I don't think I want it.'

'What?' retorts Bruce. 'My contact assured me that a promotion was just the thing to lure you. You're known to be ambitious.'

'Am I? I guess I have been chasing that goal. But I've recently had a realisation, very recently actually. I care about something else just as much as my own promotion. I care about the quality of the whole team in which I work. And it strikes me that if JumboJumbo just promotes people to keep them happy and they have no regard for capability or merit, then that's not going to be a super-star team. Is it?'

Bruce draws breath but doesn't offer a rebuttal, so Caroline forges ahead. 'I want to sincerely thank you for contacting me, but over the next few months I'm going to be really working hard to demonstrate to my team that promotion isn't the only thing that motivates me. *Our* success motivates me. That feels the right focus for me right now.'

A few muttered niceties and Bruce hangs up. Bruce knew he was going to have to work incredibly hard to pull Caroline away now.

Caroline leans back and feels the anger and injustice leave her. With a small smile, she welcomes in their place a rosy glow of pride in her ability to see a new truth, one that is beyond herself. She reaches for her sunglasses and heads over to join the crowd.

Don't worry. Caroline the Co-Pilot will use her middle name, Patsy, in future. Patsy the Pilot!

Your turn at the controls

Notice in our story that Caroline does not consciously appear to reflect. And yet we can see there is an outcome that has arisen from unconscious reflection. At some point the various interactions in our story have come together for her to generate a new and previously unexpected outcome. This indicates the value of reflection and increases the importance of actively undertaking this activity. Both for yourself and for others.

 FLYING STRAIGHT AND LEVEL

1. Print out the quote 'Insanity is doing the same thing over and over again and expecting different results' and pin it on the wall or make it your screensaver. Each time you look at it ask yourself if you have reflected recently.

2. Practise your personal reflection processes with each of the following:
   - Go for a walk during office hours.
   - On your commute home (if you are not driving).
   - Over lunch – turn off your computer and mobile devices and sit alone.
   - In the shower or bath.

   Try your own variation. Make notes on how each of these felt and which seems most effective for you. We all have our preferences.

3. Build in reflection to your meetings with individuals and with your team and ask:
   - What did we learn today that surprised us?
   - What did we learn today that altered our view of the world?
   - What fundamental assumptions are we making about the competitive environment or business context that could be wrong?
   - What values are we taking for granted? What other values might change this situation for us?

4. Practise reflection on yourself to deeply understand the assumptions you hold that drive your behaviour. Make this the goal of your reflective learning. Use the 'why' questioning technique in your private journal. Repeat until you feel entirely comfortable with this approach to deep reflection – and then carry on.

 ## LOOPING THE LOOP

1. Ask your team members how they reflect on their work:

   - This could be explored openly in a team meeting if there is sufficient trust so that people feel comfortable to share and learn together. Compare approaches. Ask questions to tease out whether this reflection process is active or passive.

   - Be ready for the possibility that some colleagues may have never considered such a question before and hence may not know their answer yet.

2. Build in questions to your coaching conversations that ask about assumptions. Remember that this may be challenging to your coachees so take care with contracting and gaining permission:

   - What is your assumption?
   - What belief leads you to that conclusion?
   - What values do you hold that drive that behaviour?

3. Help people to look in the mirror and see for themselves how they become fixed in their views because of assumptions they hold:

   - What holds that belief fixed?
   - What would happen if you didn't believe that?
   - What other value do you hold just as dearly that might allow you to try something else?

THINGS TO DO BEFORE THE
NEXT FLIGHT

Read about Chris Argyris' 'Double Loop Learning' in the *Harvard Business Review*: we provide a link on our website

Read Terry Borton's '*Reach, Teach and Touch*', published in 1970 by McGraw Hill, London.

For further resources go to: www.coachingonthego.co.uk

Part **3**

The Pilot's manual

On-the-Go

PILOT'S MANUAL

Coaching *On-the-Go*

Welcome. So far we have taught you how to fly and now we're going to teach you how to look after your new plane. Well, that might be stretching the metaphor just a little bit. We have shared with you all the tools that we find ourselves using on a daily basis, if not on an hourly basis. And you can too. These are the go-to skills of every coach we know and we have made sure that we found a way to condense those skills into ten-minute chunks so that even complex ideas can be made simple and useable really quickly.

However, there's more. Much more. We realised that as well as the tools that we use every day in our coaching, there are models and ideas that we have learnt over the years that inform our practice, that are not used every day, but our coaching would have less impact without them.

So, this part is just like a car manual: it tells you more about the fantastic machine you've purchased and it gives you a bit more detail than the glossy sales brochure. Same principle here. We're going to give you more tools and ideas to add to your coaching toolkit. These are likely to be high-impact extensions to the core skills we've already covered, and probably used less regularly.

Each chapter is written to offer you ten-minute chunks along with stand-alone activities that you can explore to enhance your skills *On-the-Go*. Some of these will demonstrate the considerable overlap between coaching and general leadership skills. These skills play an important role in effective coaching and often represent opportunities to boost the impact of your leadership capabilities too. For those of you interested to take these skills even further, we also outline what it takes to become a professionally accredited coach.

First, we give you some cool tools to help you know yourself better. After that, we show you how you can use some tools with your coachees so that they can get to know themselves better. Then we offer a chapter with tools that have been of huge importance to us in our coaching careers. Then we turn to a question that you might reflect on: 'How's it going?' Great question. We provide guidance to help you assess your impact. Then, if any of this coaching has whetted your appetite for more, we introduce you to a range of professional coaching bodies where you can learn more.

Departures

TIME	DESTINATION	FLIGHT	GATE	REMARKS

More about You

More about OTHERS

More great TOOLS

More about IS IT WORKING?

More about PROFESSIONAL COACHING

Chapter **12**

More about YOU

Your leadership

We invite you to answer the questions below.

UNIQUE ★
IN THE COACHING MARKET

- How did you learn to be a leader?
- Who do you have in your life that you model your leadership on?
- What is it about them that leads you to model them?
- How do you know that your chosen leadership style is effective?
- When do you change your leadership style?
- What prompts you to change it?

Please reflect on your answers and record them – type them up or write them down. Your answers will help you better engage with some of the material we present here. Remember that this process of reflection will generate greater development opportunities that are personal to you.

Often, we're not taught formally to be a leader, and we've picked it up in bits and pieces along the way. Other people can be a source of inspiration in both a positive and negative way: 'I aspire to being like her,' or 'I really don't want to be that sort of leader.' Some of us have had the benefit of a graduate school where we can attend leadership lectures, but as we get into the thick of things it becomes quickly apparent that the theory may be wildly different from the practice.

If you're curious about different ways to think about being a leader, there are some really useful models that help map the different aspects of leadership. These include an important role for coaching. And these are most particularly useful when we consider the last two questions above: whether you change your style of leadership, and if so, how you know when to flex it.

Which leads us to address a prevailing leadership myth. When we talk in our workshops to people about flexing their leadership style, many people are concerned that they remain authentic. Their belief is that any variation in leadership style might be seen as inauthentic. An alternative view, we think, is that it is entirely possible to have a reliable set of values which you can be transparent about (that's the authentic bit), but to also have a behavioural repertoire that allows you to respond consciously in an appropriate way in different circumstances (that's the flexible bit). If you're a leader in the US, some of your leadership behaviours might be entirely inappropriate in Russia or Indonesia (and vice versa). That's why it is imperative that you learn how to flex *On-the-Go*, while staying true to your deep personal values.

Research tells us that this ability to read a situation and flex your style is career-critical when changing country cultures, as described above. But what is often unacknowledged is how critical this can be when you stay within a country culture, but you change company or even divisional cultures. The statistics are stark: very few leaders who are top performers in one company manage to sustain the top performance status when they move. This is because we over-attribute performance to one person and under-attribute performance within a context which includes knowledge networks, organisational navigation know-how and personal professional capital.

In short, your leadership will benefit from an appreciation and self-aware-ness of your model of leadership. This will benefit your ability to maximise the impact of the coaching skills you developed through the application of Part 2 The main flight.

The situational leadership model *On-the-Go*

The situational leadership model dates back to the late 1960s, but because it makes intuitive sense it remains a firm favourite to help think about what aspects of leading are important. And coaching has a central role in the model. The model's authors, Hersey and Blanchard, updated the model in the 1980s and the updated version is shown below.

The model proposes four styles of leading: directing, coaching, supporting and delegating. While there are some academic criticisms and limitations of this model, many people agree that there are helpful things you can explore with it to enhance your leadership and coaching skills. We see value in this model from three perspectives:

- First, it states there is no one way to be an effective leader and that leading includes an element of responding to a set of circumstances.

- Second, it draws attention to the possibility that you may adjust your leadership style for the same individual if the circumstances change.

- Third, it introduces the concept of leaders adopting a coaching style as an effective way of leading. Indeed, a transformational style.

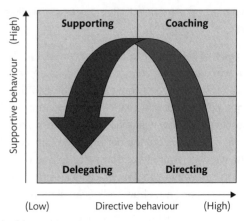

Situational leadership

Source: Hersey-Blanchard Situational Leadership® Theory.

The model proposes that the type of task being undertaken, in combination with the level of the individual's developmental maturity in relation to that task, determines the style of leader that will be most effective. The model advocates that a combination of directive and supportive leadership styles is appropriate depending upon the competence and commitment of the individuals.

In other words, if the individuals are entirely new to a task, having not done anything similar before, this implies reduced levels of competence or capability. If at the same time they lack commitment to the task perhaps through a lack of confidence, then a leader can consider being directive in their style. This is the right-hand corner of the matrix. At the other extreme, where the individuals have considerable existing competence for a task and are highly committed to it, perhaps through experience or self-motivation, a leader can delegate as much as possible, allowing the individuals to determine how to go about the task in its entirety, subject to the required delivery outcomes. To give an extremely basic example, when a new starter joins your organisation fresh from college you usually tell them where the toilets are (directive); we don't leave them to work it out for themselves (delegation).

Arguably, the end point that all leaders want to be in is that of delegation. Empowering your team, which ultimately gives you more time for strategic issues. You will see that the first step to move from the directive position to this desired goal is a coaching style of leadership. The model advocates that, using the many skills we have presented in this book, a leader uses coaching to help someone identify how to address a task for themselves, while still being supported and guided. The coaching process builds the confidence and commitment of the individual. As their capability to address uncertain and new activities develops, so the level of direction you need to give reduces and hence a focus on supporting behaviour is more appropriate. Essentially this means making sure they have the support when they need it.

Your turn at the controls

If you've never thought about how you learnt to be a leader, now is the time. Or, if you have been on courses about leadership, now is a good time to reflect on whether what you learned really did shape how you lead or whether you have put some concepts aside. Consider too whether you'd like to read or listen to some podcasts on leadership so that you get more exposure to ideas on the subject.

 FLYING STRAIGHT AND LEVEL

1. Create a list of the key tasks that each of your team members performs. If you run more than one team, for example, project teams as well as departmental teams, apply this to each such team. ▶

- For each individual, identify their level of competence and commitment towards each of these key tasks and hence which boxes in the matrix above they fall into. In other words, identify the appropriate type of leadership behaviour you might consider providing them with.

- Now check what evidence you have that you are providing the most appropriate leadership behaviours at the right times.

- Identify what steps you should take to change your behaviour for each identified key task.

2. Share your thinking with each team member and seek their feedback. Be ready to use your feedback skills to explain how you have allocated the key tasks. Ask each team member how they would like your behaviours to change.

3. Change your behaviours

4. And reflect on what happens.

5. And repeat.

 LOOPING THE LOOP

1. Repeat the exercise above with respect to the work that you do for your boss:

   - Assess how your boss's behaviours vary depending on the activities that you undertake.

   - What do you observe about the patterns of behaviour relative to task. Do you see places where you might ask for more delegation or more direction?

   - Take these observations (probably in the form of questions) into your next one-to-one session with your boss.

2. Look back at your answers to the questions at the start of this chapter.

   - Identify how the situational leadership model applies to the behaviours of your role models and those that taught you your leadership skills.

   - What do you learn from this?

The Johari Window *On-the-Go*

Here's another 2x2 model: the Johari Window. The standard original model uses four windows to explain different levels of self-awareness and self-disclosure. The assumption is that you can know some things about yourself but don't know other things. And that others can know some things about you, but not other things. This creates your personal four windows:

- Arena – things are known by you and known by others.

- Blind spot – things others can see about you and you don't know.

- Façade – things you know about yourself, and you don't reveal them to others.

- Unknown – things about you that neither you nor others know.

Johari Window

The Johari Window

As a leader, the façade window is a difficult place to be because we can pretend to be one way, but in times of stress or under pressure, the 'real us' reveals itself. This is why self-awareness is considered so imperative for leaders because higher levels of self-awareness suggest that both the blind spot and the unknown can become smaller windows.

Unlike other models, the theory that sits behind this one suggests that the vertical and horizontal axes can shift, thereby opening up bigger windows of self-knowledge or self-disclosure. Thus, a blind spot (and unknown) can be reduced (but never omitted) by the skilful use of feedback. The other behaviour 'self-disclosure' is akin to concepts of authenticity whereby leaders share information designed to increase mutual understanding. This offers a role to learn more about yourself as well as a rationale for coaching your teams to grow their own self-awareness.

Finally, we suggest there is a link between your approach to the size of your arena – the extent to which you are open when sharing personal issues with others at work – and building trust with your team. Patrick Lencioni refers to this as 'being vulnerable'. A willingness to share your vulnerabilities with others is a cornerstone of building trust and hence generating an effective team.

Your turn at the controls

We all consider ourselves far more self-aware than we are. Sadly, the more senior you are, the more difficult it can be to hear how you 'show up' to others. This is one reason perhaps why leaders can suffer from excessive self-confidence. Here are some ideas to stop you falling into this trap.

 FLYING STRAIGHT AND LEVEL

1. Draw your own Venn diagram showing the overlaps between:

- How well your family knows you (your friends and work).
- How well your friends know you (your family and work).
- How well your work colleagues – consider splitting this into senior and junior colleagues – know you (your family and friends).

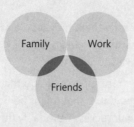

Example of a Venn diagram

In this example, you might wonder why more of your friends don't know more about your family, or you might ponder why there is no overlap between work and family – and isn't that interesting and you may feel entirely appropriate too. But your diagram may be different and raise different questions.

2. Now repeat this exercise as best you can for a work colleague or leader you know well and who you consider to be a role model.

3. How well does your approach serve you?

4. How does your approach differ to that of your role model? What might explain this difference – contextual issues perhaps? What changes does this suggest you might take?

5. Make those changes.

6. Look back at your Venn diagram. Take one thing that your family or friends know that it would be appropriate to share with your work colleagues in an authentic way.

   • How would it make you feel to share this?

   • What stops you?

   • What are the benefits or downsides to sharing this much of yourself?

7. Think about the following scenario:

   You're going to eavesdrop on a discussion between your mother or father and your very best friend in the whole world. They're talking about you: what you're great at, what you're not great at, your hot buttons, your soft spots, your likes and dislikes, your way of communicating when you are tired or upset.

▶

- What do you honestly think they would say? What are the things they might say that make you go 'ouch'? What are the things they might say that make your heart sing?

- Now think about those aspects of you that might be important at work. These are the things that might be holding you back or they might be part of your success – probably they are part of both these things. What insight does this exercise give you on your leadership?

 LOOPING THE LOOP

1. Now that you have worked with the Johari Window on yourself, share with your coachees why you found the process helpful and ask if they would like to try.

2. Next time you are coaching someone, pay attention to the things about them that you're acutely aware of, but you sense that they are not aware of.

   - Draw the Johari Window for them and ask them to put one or two key words in three windows: arena, blind spot and façade.

   - Explore with them what they have placed in each window and how it might be helping or hindering them in their role.

   - If they say that there might be things they are blind to, that they would benefit from learning, jointly design a way for them to get helpful, supportive and insightful feedback on themselves.

   - If they ask you to contribute to that feedback, share with them what you observe.

3. Next time you have a team meeting where it is appropriate for the team to do some learning together, draw the Johari Window and describe what it is and how it works.

   - Invite questions from the team to help them fully understand the model.

   - Propose a series of rotating one-to-one conversations. The target is that everyone gets to speak to everyone else (at least 15 minutes per rotation), although if there isn't enough time you could do it over a series of meetings.

   - Have blank templates of the window as a handout.

- Collaboratively design some 'insight rules' as a group that identify how you will work together, for example, respectful listening, confidentiality, phrasing things in a way that is clear but gentle, limiting the amount of feedback the team provides to each other so as not to overwhelm anyone.

- Start the conversations and rotate: five minutes person A gives insight into person B's windows; five minutes swap; five minutes as a pair discussing and comparing; take a Pause-Point™.

- Have plenty of time as a team to debrief at the end of all the rotations

    a. What did people notice?

    b. What did people learn that they want to share?

- Offer support to every individual who may want to process what they have heard, make sure you are available for people to talk to about this exercise afterwards and actively offer such support in a coaching manner. Your next one-to-one would be an ideal place and time to do this.

THINGS TO DO BEFORE THE NEXT FLIGHT

Situational leadership is a very simplistic model with a simple set of contingencies and there has been much academic discussion about its accuracy. For a full review of the model read Claude L Graeff's article from 1983 'The situational leadership theory: A critical view' in *Academy of Management Review, 8*(2), pp. 285–291.

Read Patrick M Lencioni's *'The Five Dysfunctions of a Team: A Leadership Fable'*, published in 2006 by John Wiley & Sons.

Watch one or more of the many videos on YouTube where Patrick Lencioni shares his insights. We provide links on our website.

For further resources go to: www.coachingonthego.co.uk

Chapter **13**

More about
OTHERS

How to coach self-awareness

Earlier in this book we looked at some psychometric profiling tools. There is an extremely wide range of such tools and they are widely used in the organisational recruitment process across the Anglo-Saxon world and increasingly elsewhere.

When a team is seen to be under-performing, or budget is provided for some team development work, these psychometric tests are often used with the aim of helping people to understand themselves and those around them. Furthermore, when professional coaches are hired to work with leaders to improve their capabilities and effectiveness, they regularly commence the process by using some form of psychometric test, often based on 360° feedback, with which to explore the client's self-awareness and identify what areas to focus on. And yet there are immense challenges regarding these tools.

At its simplest, it is easy to argue that psychometric tools should only be used by those with the skills and training to do so. However, in our professional experience we come across many occasions where this doesn't really work. Often because organisations do not invest enough in the process, but also because the tests fundamentally tell us what we want to hear. After all, we love to hear about ourselves and have our biases confirmed.

Which is why confirmation bias is a problem. This is a widely researched and widely acknowledged phenomenon where people interpret information, search for data or recall information that confirms their existing beliefs. And so ignore other data. If, for example, you have spent your childhood being told by your elders and betters that you are an extravert, there is a good chance you will believe this by taking note of evidence that supports such an idea and ignoring the evidence that challenges it. Once you see yourself as an extravert it is difficult to find evidence that points to the opposite. (If you want to illustrate the impact of confirmation bias to your colleagues, check out the Asch Experiment below.)

Context is another crucial impact. Many of the psychometric tools acknowledge this, identifying that the context might change the findings. This might include when working under stress or not, or when at work versus at play. Phil has a very personal story to share to illustrate this. When working as finance director in a large private-sector IT business, the executive team of which he was a member all completed a particular psychometric tool. Its findings were based around three core preferences: a preference for data/analysis, a preference to complete tasks and a preference to support people.

The findings for Phil strongly suggested he had a preference to support people. His team colleagues openly laughed and mocked the results when these findings were shared. 'This tool is rubbish' said one colleague. 'Phil is the one we all rely on because he constantly makes sure we hit our financial numbers and drives us to achieve this month by month.' Phil was nearly brought to tears as he explained that he did this as it was what the job and organisational culture demanded of him, but it was not him. Fortunately, he had that insight. Indeed, it was part of the journey that changed his career.

Nevertheless, some tests provide useful insight to the people taking them and some tests have more rigour than others. As many of these tools are commercially available, without being licensed to use them (having been specifically trained), you may find it difficult to access them. Some would argue that the *best* tools are secure behind these firewalls, which tries to guarantee a standard of interpretation and debriefing from trained psychologists or coaches.

We're not convinced that paying large amounts of money to be accredited in these tests guarantees better quality, but if this is something you feel that you would benefit knowing about, we do encourage you to research the wide range of tests available and really investigate the assertions they make about reliability and validity (the two most important assessments of a test's accuracy). Do not take popularity as the measure of success.

There are some free tests on the internet. The ones below were identified in 2019 when this book was published. Access may change and yet if you search we anticipate there will still be other versions available for free.

www.16personalities.com

https://testyourself.psychtests.com/testid/3113

https://www.mindtools.com/

Your turn at the controls

Here are some suggestions to help you use psychometric tools and the principles behind them in your coaching.

 FLYING STRAIGHT AND LEVEL

We advocate taking steps without using psychometric tools, and yet using the principles often used in these tools, to identify your strengths and weaknesses. This is with a view to maximising the use of the former (and yet not overplaying them) and managing and improving the latter.

1. Seek feedback from colleagues. If your company has a 360-degree feedback process, embrace it and use it to really learn about yourself. Also make use of less formal channels to ask for feedback. Ask direct questions, listen attentively, and don't justify your actions. Reflect on what you have heard and identify actions to change.

2. Create your own process for reflection:
   - Write down key decisions and the motivations that influenced them in the last 12 months. Note any assumptions you made.
   - After 6 to 12 months, go back and re-examine your decisions, particularly finding the ways your assumptions were accurate or misguided.

3. Admit mistakes. Admitting to a mistake is a sign of strength, not weakness. You are not authentic when you ignore mistakes or allow blame to fall on someone else.

4. Particularly, think about strengths that you have that are under-used in your current role and how you might use them more.

5. Think about your natural talents that are underdeveloped and ways that you might do that.

6. Take steps to change.

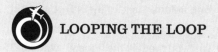

LOOPING THE LOOP

With any of these psychometric tools, we believe that by taking a coaching approach you can work with them to improve your own understanding of yourself or to help colleagues understand themselves, and in both cases find ways to improve your skills and capabilities. You do this by continuously asking questions of the information that the tests provide to challenge and learn from – and by proactively avoiding the assumption that the findings of the test are accurate or correct in any way. These processes require you to invest time in the tool and its use. And yet once you have started to explore it, you will find its usefulness as a reference point can apply as you work with your coachee *On-the-Go*.

Ways to start the questioning process include:

1. Before looking at the findings of the tool, help your coachee to describe what they expect it to say and give evidence as to why.

    a. Given that most tools are extensive, this is a long activity.

    b. Use your coaching skills to question what is said and to identify what your coachee would like to change.

    c. Have your coachee note down a summary of all their expectations including any developments or changes from your coaching.

    d. You may want to offer your own expectations on what the findings might be for your coachee depending upon your leadership relationship with them. Of course, this will require careful management and use of our feedback models.

2. The next stage is to review what the tool says and take a generic approach to each of the findings. For example, if a tool reports that you have a tendency or a preference to, for example – act strategically and avoid the detail.

    a. What evidence do you have that would prove this to be incorrect?

    b. What evidence do you have that this describes you as distinct to your colleagues?

    c. What is there about your current context that makes this outcome more likely than in another context?

▶

   d. How does this compare to your preferred style or the way you would like to be recognised?

   e. How does this compare to what you thought the findings would be?

3. What would you like to change and how can I help you?

Transactional Analysis *On-the-Go*

Just as some coaches lean heavily on personality tests, others use frameworks such as Transactional Analysis (TA). We think these are all useful tools to have in your kitbag, but be cautious when you find yourself using the same ones all the time. It's much more important to be alive to the coachee and their situation, fully present, listening and with great questions than being smart with too many tools or models. With that caveat in place, let's look at TA.

Transactional Analysis has crossed over to the coaching world from the psychoanalytic profession and with that transition there is a faint whiff of a problem. In psychoanalysis there is *analysis* whereas in coaching there is none. This is an important distinction. As a coach, our role is never to analyse anyone or to suggest to them that we know them better than they know themselves. Consider the Johari Window: we may see behaviour or aspects of them they don't see but this is **not** analysis.

So as a coach using TA, you might like to offer this as another model that can be helpful for the coachee to do their own analysis of the situation or relationship. There is a considerable wealth of additional material available on TA. Our aim here is to share a small amount that you can use to great effect if you want to. As with everything in this book, we encourage you to play with this concept and judge its usefulness to you, your style and the context within which you work.

In TA, people are said to be able to occupy three ego-states: Parent, Adult and Child. These states are not correlated with an individual's maturity, so a 50-year old is still able to occupy the Child state. What determines your current state is whether you're in-the-moment experience is being shaped by 'thinking' (Adult), patterns or rules that you've been 'taught' (Parent), or the simple 'raw' experience such as seeing, hearing and feeling (Child). Other interpretations of these three states are simpler and suggest that the Adult state is what's appropriate to you now as an adult, the Child state is what you experienced as a child and the Parent state represents what you learnt as you were growing up. These states are usually represented as shown below.

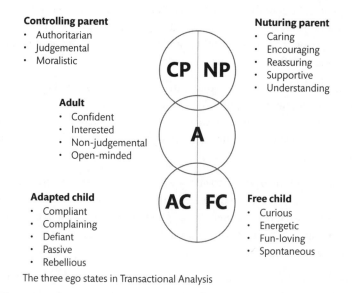

Controlling parent
- Authoritarian
- Judgemental
- Moralistic

Nuturing parent
- Caring
- Encouraging
- Reassuring
- Supportive
- Understanding

Adult
- Confident
- Interested
- Non-judgemental
- Open-minded

Adapted child
- Compliant
- Complaining
- Defiant
- Passive
- Rebellious

Free child
- Curious
- Energetic
- Fun-loving
- Spontaneous

The three ego states in Transactional Analysis

Each of the three ego-states is a bundle of attitudes, patterns of thinking and fixed points of view. Each ego-state has both a positive intention and potentially a negative intention. Sometimes we forget about the positive intention. When people are communicating (whether verbal or otherwise), each party is said to be in one of the ego-states and, broadly speaking, if there is a difference or mismatch this can reduce the positive outcomes. Furthermore, there is also the distinction regarding how each of us sees our own position in the world in terms of our inner voice. Is it being child-like suggesting that we act sulkily in response to an issue, or adult-like addressing it in a way that seeks an acceptable solution?

The ideal state for coaching is for both the coach and the coachee to be in the Adult ego-state. This means that both are feeling okay about themselves and each other. And their emotions and attitudes are positive, enabling them to have an Adult-to-Adult conversation, both responding rationally and believing in each other and themselves.

And it is also possible for the coachee to feel more like a child, either defensive and cross or playful. The coach can go there too and help the coachee get out of that stuck place, and release some of their frustration or emotion and begin to see the world from a better place, where they can stop blaming themselves or others and can take a more Adult or rational view and shift their 'stuckness'.

Coach or coachee can also go into the Parent ego-state, either a helpful parent or a controlling one. TA can be useful in coaching in helping us recognise what ego-state we're in and our coachee is in – and then take steps to shift our states into an ego-state that is more helpful to moving on.

In coaching we help people to notice where they may have been or tend to go in a conversation (with others or in their heads) and hence to consider and notice what may happen if they go elsewhere. For example, is there something a colleague says that always triggers you to go into a childish mode which is not helpful?

Some coaches use the three states as a way of checking with their coachee about their current state or the state in which they've found themselves in when in difficult situations. The other common use for TA is to think about the types of communication that are most helpful to you. Again very simply, if someone is embodied in the Parent state, then it helps to use language and concepts with them that chime with that state.

Another tool derived from TA is the Drama Triangle and its more positive variation, the Winner's Triangle. Each of these is shown below.

The drama triangle and the winner's triangle

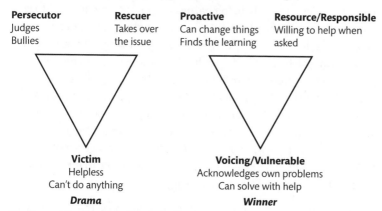

Persecutor	**Rescuer**	**Proactive**	**Resource/Responsible**
Judges	Takes over	Can change things	Willing to help when
Bullies	the issue	Finds the learning	asked

Victim
Helpless
Can't do anything
Drama

Voicing/Vulnerable
Acknowledges own problems
Can solve with help
Winner

The Drama Triangle and the Winner's Triangle

In the Drama Triangle, the idea is that people can find themselves in one of three unhelpful places when interacting with others or reflecting in their heads with their inner voices. These three roles are:

- Victim – I'm being hard done by and I'm helpless to change it.

- Rescuer – I'm only trying to help and sort out the problem for you.

- Persecutor – They should do it my way, then everything will be alright.

How can the roles become more effective? Each of the Drama Triangle roles has a valid aspect: the victim has a problem which needs to be solved, the rescuer feels a real concern for others and the persecutor wants to put limits on what is expected of them. To make these real in a positive way, new strategies are required which we see in the Winner's Triangle:

- The victim needs to voice their feelings and acknowledge their vulner-ability. Talk to any others involved honestly and start to work on solving the problem.

- The persecutor needs to become proactive and start to define bound-aries. Then work with others by focusing on what they are good at and the times that they have successfully dealt with that particular situation.

- The rescuer needs to become responsible and support others in doing what they need to and stop doing things for others.

While there is considerably more depth and learning available about TA, these triangles can really help coachees when they are feeling stuck or unclear about what may be affecting their behaviour. The coachee can be asked to identify where they currently are in the triangle: 'I'm expressing a situation in which I simply do not think I know what to do next with this project, so I suppose in terms of this model I'm feeling like a victim'. And then ask what steps they could take if they were to move to the relevant corner of the Winner's Triangle: 'Okay, so I suppose specifically I do not know how to evaluate the finances, where to find extra resources, nor how to tell the client that we are behind.' While this is a simple example, it illustrates how a shift in mindset can help to identify steps to move forward, which is the underlying aim of coaching.

You can anticipate that coachees may identify how they are moving around the triangles and sitting in different positions at the same time. All of this can help them break down their challenges and identify how they might work differently. And you can draw on this tool when coaching *On-the-Go* by simply drawing attention to what you hear. You might say to your coachee, 'I hear you describing how you're feeling almost bullied into the choices you're making. Does that sound fair? What would happen if you imagined standing up and defending your position, looking for actions that might reverse this feeling?'

Your turn at the controls

This set of tools helps your coachee to relate to themselves in new ways.

 ### FLYING STRAIGHT AND LEVEL

1. In meetings, begin to observe who is in Child, Parent or Adult state.
   - Note who communicates and adjusts their communication to take account of these different states.

- Notice what states are most effective with different people. Does the playful child trigger one person to action? Does another person prefer the direction of a parental style?

2. Set some time aside to consider your team members or key colleagues. What tendencies do they have to sit in different positions in the Drama and Winner's Triangles?

  - Do you have colleagues that never complete their own tasks as they spend too much time rescuing other people?

  - Do you have team members who could benefit from occasionally rescuing colleagues? (Each corner of the triangle is not 100% unhelpful.)

 LOOPING THE LOOP

1. With a coachee, talk through an interaction where they want to gain an insight by explaining the Parent, Adult and Child constructs and asking who was in which state during the various points of the interaction. What triggered any changes? What state would you prefer to be in next time?

  Notice the focus here is to maintain a forward-looking agenda in line with the philosophy of coaching rather than an analytical backward-looking focus.

2. Try the three chairs exercise described at the end of Chapter 7 and ask your coachee to talk through a situation from chair 1 in Child state, chair 2 in Parent state and chair 3 in Adult state. Explore the differences they notice and experience.

3. With a coachee who appears stuck with a question, use the Drama and Winner's Triangles. Explain the principles, possibly illustrate how they work with an example of your own experience that your coachee may recognise and ask them to explore the question with the use of the triangle.

  - If you have someone you think might enjoy a more visceral experience, use a flipchart to draw out the triangles on the floor and move round the points physically as you explore the question at hand.

  - Assist the coachee to find new ways forward.

THINGS TO DO BEFORE THE NEXT FLIGHT

Read about or do the Asch Experiment: there is a link on our website.

Read Ian Stewart and Vann Joines 'TA Today: A New Introduction to Transactional Analysis', published in 1987 by Vann Joines.

Read Acey Choy's 'The winner's triangle' in Transactional Analysis Journal, 20 (1), pp. 40–46, 1968.

Read Stephen Karpman's 'Fairy tales and script drama analysis' in Transactional Analysis Bulletin, 7 (26), pp. 39–43.

Read Stan Woollams and Michael Brown's 'Transactional Analysis: A Modern and Comprehensive text of TA Theory and Practice', published by Dexter, MI: Huron Valley Institute in 1978.

For further resources go to: www.coachingonthego.co.uk

Chapter **14**

More great TOOLS

More GREAT TOOLS and how to coach with them

Questions and questions-about-questions

When you're coaching someone else, you are acting as a thinking partner. Your questions are imperative to the process of thinking together. Some questions are more powerful than others because they quite simply require answers that reveal more – deeper, hidden thinking. Powerful questions often generate long silences or Pause-Points™ such as 'That's a great question'. Also watch out for the unconscious attempt to avoid the question: 'Wow, what made you think of that question?' Be a strong coach and keep them focused.

The simplest way to figure out whether you are asking a powerful question is to look at this hierarchy.

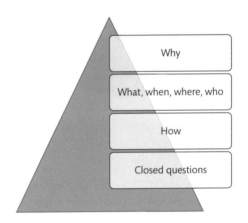

Question hierarchy

Generally, questions that start with a 'why' are considered the most powerful. But hold on there. Don't rush to a why question just yet. There is a small problem we've found with using why in some situations and it is this: it can feel very challenging. It can feel like you're asking someone to *justify* their thinking, not just explain or share their thinking.

Instead, we find that 'what' questions can be equally powerful without the risks of defensiveness. So, go ahead, ask all the what questions you can. What was motivating you to do that? What was your thinking behind that decision? What did you hope to achieve?

There are other equally powerful, open-ended questions in the pyramid. Helpfully they also start with 'w' (that's our own personal rule of thumb). All open-ended questions require the other person to share their world view and that's what you want to understand most as a coach. How do they see the world or how do they see this issue?

We both want to point out that this pyramid is simply an easy framework to aid memory, and is not cast in stone. Phil particularly disagrees with relegating 'how' questions to a lower level. His argument is that they often move the conversation from content to behaviour and as such it is a very powerful format. For example: How did that make you feel? or How will you do that?

Powerful questions can also be really creative questions. In a workshop exercise that we regularly run, people can only ask each other questions. Some of the best questions don't ask about logic or rationale but tap into other aspects of an individual's psyche. Here's a selection of some of the best we've heard:

- What would you do if you had a magic wand?

- What would your dad/mum/best friend/kids say?

- How do you know?

- What would happen if you couldn't resolve this?

- What are you really afraid of?

- And?

- What would happen if you did nothing?

And do not forget the silent question: looking your coachee directly in the eye and raising your eyebrows, shrugging your shoulders or opening your hands.

The last question above, by the way, Phil says is the favourite question of a finance professional when you are asking for more money. Always be prepared to answer this when you want more budget.

Needless to say, the least powerful questions are closed, where the question only offers a limited number of responses. The most obvious is when grammatically someone can only answer yes or no to what you've asked: Did you deliver the report on time? Less obvious examples give a series of options: Did you deliver the report yesterday or today?

Closed questions can be useful in some situations, just don't overuse them. Look out for your preferred language when operating *On-the-Go*. An example of a useful closed question might be to draw something to your coachee's attention: 'You just said you delivered the report on time. Was that on time in your opinion or the client's opinion?'

When you have great rapport with your coachee and you are used to working together in this way, the coachee will probably ignore a closed question and answer in the most appropriate way. However, we invite you to notice your closed questions so that you use them intentionally and not just habitually.

Your turn at the controls

Here are some ways to practise powerful questions. Also, in case you are wondering why some of your great questions don't have much impact, let us quickly remind you that as with everything in coaching 'it is in the eyes of the beholder'. In other words, your questions are only powerful if they are received as powerful by your coachee. Watching carefully what moves your coachee to new insights will show you which questions are being received as powerful.

FLYING STRAIGHT AND LEVEL

1. Think of someone you would like to engage with in a coaching conversation: think about people above you, below you and alongside you in the hierarchy.

2. Set your timer for five minutes.

3. With that person in mind, spend five minutes writing down all the most powerful questions that you can possibly think about for a current situation involving that person.

4. At the end of five minutes, identify the questions you think are likely to be most powerful (notice any closed questions too).

5. In your remaining five minutes think about how you might integrate these questions into your next conversation.

A powerful question makes you and others think more deeply. Start noticing great questions that other people ask.

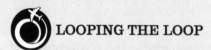 **LOOPING THE LOOP**

Repeat the above exercise and apply it to the following scenarios:

1. Your boss has over-ruled a decision you took previously, and you feel undermined by their actions.

2. One of your team members is demonstrating a lack of motivation and commitment.

3. A peer of yours is overwhelmed by workload, stressed and is not prioritising well.

If you are going to take this exercise and use it in conversation with others, don't forget to do some contracting at the beginning: 'Hi, can we spend some time revisiting xxx. I'd appreciate understanding your thinking' or 'Hi, we seem to be working in different ways and I'd like to understand what's going on. Do you have 30 minutes?'

▶

Now deploy really great, powerful questions, such as:

- What had I overlooked when I decided. . . ?

- What did you see that I didn't?

- What do I need to be aware of in the future?

- What's giving you job satisfaction?

- What does a 'great day at work' look like for you?

SBI feedback model

Offering feedback is a significant role that the effective coach plays. It is also a significant role in leadership. And, finally, helping to develop other people's abilities to accept and act upon feedback is also an important activity for a coach when working with a coachee. We have offered our own feedback model, STARTER™.

There is another powerful feedback model that we would like to share with you, the SBI model. Its simplicity makes it attractive and it can help you and your coachees build their awareness. While it requires practice, it can soon become second nature and ready for you to use *On-the-Go*.

The SBI model stands for Situation, Behaviour, Impact and was created by the Center for Creative Leadership. And as with the STARTER™ model, it works for all types of feedback – inspirational, developmental, negative and positive.

The first step, and possibly the easiest, is the 'S' of situation – the specific situation in which the event happened about which you wish to give feedback. It's important to describe this so that the recipient knows exactly what you are talking about in order to consider amending their actions or behaviours. 'You get really passionate in meetings' is too vague. 'On Wednesday morning, in the meeting with the project team, when talking with Peter, Ahmed and Guri about the positive impact we're going to have' makes it clear. In this example you may need to be even more specific regarding what was said, which takes us to the 'B' of Behaviour.

Key to the SBI model is the ability to disaggregate behaviour from the impact that it has. The way we teach people to get this idea is to get them to imagine a video camera in the corner of the room. The video doesn't capture meaning, rather it captures action. The video only sees behaviour. By thinking about behaviour as the centre of the feedback, we avoid investing meaning to that behaviour. Most importantly, it avoids attributing to the other person their intention, feeling or thinking. For example, crossing your arms across your body is the behaviour that the video camera sees. Different people might have very different motivations for crossing their arms. Unlike in pop psychology, it might not be out of defensiveness, but because you're cold and this posture preserves body heat, or it might be because you're bored and this posture is showing disengagement.

We run into trouble when we attribute a behaviour to a thought or a feeling. Keep to the behaviour and the consequences that you identified. And allow the other person to say what motivated that behaviour. This is what the SBI model guides us to do. It may also help to think of the behaviour as the action that you see or hear: 'When you sat forward in your chair, raised your voice and spread out your arms.' It is not what you feel, as that has its place in the 'I' for Impact.

As regards the impact, this uses a similar principle to that of describing the behaviour. By saying very plainly the impact on you, there is no attribution to the feelings of the recipient over which they can get into a disagreement. Your point of view is valid, and this is how you see it. Phil likes to describe this as a fact. How you felt, and indeed how you perceived that others felt as a result of the behaviour, is a fact. Your perception is reality. Even if it does not match theirs. This invites the feedback recipient to tell you how they see it.

Put the three parts of the model together. Then assemble one short paragraph with each piece in this order – Situation, Behaviour, Impact – and then your feedback can create the platform for the desired change: 'On Wednesday morning, in the meeting with the project team, you were talking with Peter, Ahmed and Guri about the positive impact we're going to have. When you sat forward in your chair, raised your voice and spread out your arms your passion was clear for everyone to see. This created positive energy for me and, I felt, for everyone in the room. This was wonderful. I'd like you to bring that passion to your work whenever you can. How do you feel about that?'

As a leader who coaches, giving feedback blurs the line between coaching and between managing. So, we would like to pause and expand this thinking further before concluding with some practical exercises.

TO COACH OR TO LEAD

There may be times when you don't know whether you should be coaching, because possibly it will be easier to simply be a boss. To try to help navigate these choices, we have come up with a diagram. It gives three choices, which depend on what the other person sees and understands.

In both pathways one and two, you have no need to give feedback. Your role is to help raise awareness and support for the coachee as they work through what happens next. Imagine you're in a meeting with a colleague, either a peer or a member of your team.

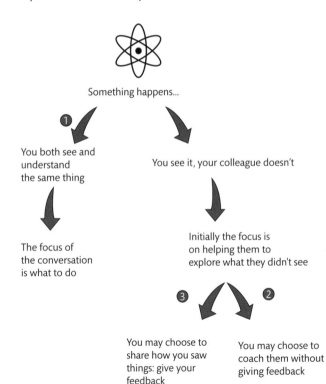

Something happens...

❶ You both see and understand the same thing

You see it, your colleague doesn't

The focus of the conversation is what to do

Initially the focus is on helping them to explore what they didn't see

❸ You may choose to share how you saw things: give your feedback

❷ You may choose to coach them without giving feedback

Feedback choices and coaching

1. The first pathway is the most obvious because the coachee has largely given themselves feedback. In this case, the coachee has enough awareness to see that the meeting or interaction didn't go as expected and that they had a part to play in that and now they are turning to you for help thinking about their next steps. The coachee has recognised a desire for change.

2. The alternative, second pathway to number one is still where the other person has sufficient awareness to figure out for themselves the 'ah ha' that something happened. They were oblivious to it at the time, but with a question or two, they come to an awareness and then your role as a coach is the same as pathway one. You have to believe in their ability to work out what the issue is for themselves, although be aware of *phoney-coaching*.

Oddly enough, *phoney-coaching* can be present when you want your colleague to do more of what they already do – you are reinforcing positive behaviour. This is because you are focused on a simple, single outcome – 'Please do more of that' – and your questions can become extremely leading. In this case pathway three, the feedback option, may be more appropriate.

3. It is the third pathway where you potentially have a conflict between coaching and managing. Of course, this is unlikely if you are seeking to reinforce positive behaviour and asking for more of it. In this case, offering direct feedback rather than coaching is likely to be a good option. You are acting here more as a line-manager or a leader. And this includes leadership towards others that you do not line-manage, nor even lead in the sense of a team.

On the other hand, an issue may require a direct feedback approach. For example, if there is insufficient time for someone to learn and adapt their behaviours and actions, perhaps to meet an immediate client demand, you are leading in a directive manner. Or where previous coaching conversations have not led to an awareness or desire to change and yet you are in a line-manager situation in which that change is a requirement. In these situations, giving direct feedback using the SBI model is a reasonable choice. The difference to our STARTER™ model is that we essentially embed the SBI approach into a broader conversation that takes a core coaching approach.

Even if you do take the approach of giving direct SBI feedback, this only presents the start of the conversation. If you find that you are on pathway three, you need to clearly contract with your coachee about giving and receiving feedback. Furthermore, you need to ask your colleague or team member to share their thinking as regards the behaviour and help them identify steps for change. And here you can bring in all the coaching skills from the rest of this book to support that process.

SBI and self-awareness

Finally, we want to add an extra layer to the SBI model to build your own self-awareness. And for this we owe thanks to a colleague and great coach Deryn Holland. When you have mapped out what you plan to say when giving feedback using the SBI model, take a Pause-Point™. And ask yourself one simple question: 'What is it about me that has brought my attention to this issue?'

This may seem like an odd question. After all, in a leadership position you are always looking for opportunities to provide developmental feedback to your team. However, we have noticed over time that it is not unusual for the trigger behind your thinking to be more about how you work and your personal preferences than it is about others. Here are a few examples:

- If you plan to give feedback that a colleague's consistent lateness at meetings is inappropriate, is this because it annoys you or because it annoys others? In many cultures, corporate and geographical, being late is the norm. It might annoy you a lot. And yet it may not matter to others.

- If you plan to give feedback that a colleague is often too pushy or too forthright when looking to close a sale, is this because you find the very process of selling uncomfortable? What evidence do you have that the behaviour is reducing sales?

- If you find yourself about to give feedback to someone who does not build and deepen stakeholder relationships enough, is this because you over-invest in relationships as a way of avoiding conflict? Does a commitment to keeping relationships intact hinder your ability to be a strong voice?

Your turn at the controls

Giving feedback lies at the very intersection of coaching and leading and is therefore a pre-eminent skill for you to become comfortable with. Take your time, and particularly develop a series of activities that will help you master this skill.

 FLYING STRAIGHT AND LEVEL

If you have not already read Chapter 2: Giving feedback, go straight to the YOUR TURN AT THE CONTROLS section and undertake the activities.

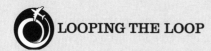

LOOPING THE LOOP

1. Identify the last four occasions when you gave a colleague feedback.

- How far back did you have to think? Does this suggest a preference to avoid conflict and hence avoid giving feedback? If so, set yourself a challenge to give feedback to at least five colleagues each month from now on. Using the one-to-one meetings advice we offer below may also help you here. And we know we are directing you here, so please consider your own targets that will be more important.

- For each of the last four times you gave feedback, review whether you followed the SBI or STARTER™ model. What learning do you take from this?

▶

2. Gather your team together and teach them the SBI model. Establish rules for the room including confidentiality. Get them to practise using the SBI model to give feedback to each other in pairs, having first thought about what they will say using the SBI model. Then get them to give feedback only on the positive behaviours that they would like to encourage. This is an easy way to practise giving feedback.

Weekly one-to-one meetings with your staff or boss

You may have previously read about and even been persuaded to implement regular one-to-one meetings with your team members. Whereby we mean those team members that you line-manage or where they are looking to you for professional development guidance. In which case, the next couple of paragraphs may just be a reminder of the significance of these meetings.

Why are we advocating this in a book about coaching skills *On-the-Go*? The answer is that while these meetings can involve a range of activities, we see their core role as the place to coach your team.

In our opinion, regular one-to-ones with your team means a weekly 30-minute session with each of your direct reports. If you can only manage every two weeks, that's a good start. If you follow the principles of these meetings, then we anticipate you will see an increase in the productivity and capability of your colleagues and hence this will more than save the time you are dedicating to these conversations.

Often, we hear people say that they do not have time for these meetings. Or that they start with good intentions and put the meetings in the diary, but have to keep cancelling them. In the latter case we ask you to consider how you would feel if your boss did the same to you – establish agreed one-to-one meeting times and then consistently cancel them as they have more important things to do than talk to you. In our coaching conversations it is not unusual to hear people describe how upset this makes them.

In addition, there are some powerful reasons to have these regular one-to-one meetings. Evidence suggests that:

- A good relationship with a leader is a more important factor in employee retention than pay or other perks. One-to-ones help you retain your best staff.

- Both individual satisfaction and productivity correlates with the individual's belief that they have a trustworthy and caring boss. One-to-ones allow you to demonstrate this.

- Retention rates rise when employees believe their managers respect their work/life balance and are willing to work with them on these issues. Wellbeing is no longer considered a nice-to-have, but an important people strategy.

- As people worry more and more about automation taking over their work, having regular conversations about development helps them to know that they are being prepared for a future world of work.

And finally, effective one-to-ones reduce the other ad hoc conversations in which your team seeks your input or advice, or you find yourself offering such support.

THE PRINCIPLES AND CONTENT OF YOUR ONE-TO-ONES

1. A regular one-to-one meeting diarised and *not cancelled* demonstrates your commitment to someone's success. It is vital that you do not consistently cancel them as this has a very negative effect.

2. Think of the meeting as an opportunity to support your team member. This is its primary purpose. In other words, think of your team member as a coachee. Identify where they need help and offer it. Do so in a coaching way. This will develop their capabilities, increase their confidence and move them to the point of maximum delegation.

3. The primary purpose of this meeting is not to give you an update on their work. This can be a secondary purpose. Many one-to-ones fail to deliver because employees expect to turn up to explain the current progress and to hear their leader tell them (yes, tell them) what to do next. The leader often thinks they are giving advice. But given their hierarchical seniority, this is interpreted as instruction. It reduces empowerment and the process whereby individuals resolve their own challenges. And they stop finding their own way – what's the point, they'll be told what to do anyway.

4. Take care if your organisation uses a project tracking methodology of traffic lights or red, amber and green systems. This involves identifying the stages of a project or overall project status as red (we have a problem), amber (we can see a problem may happen) and green (everything's on track). This risks the one-to-one meeting focusing on the red issues rather than where your team member seeks your support, advice or coaching. So, while you might need to review the traffic lights, take care to ask where they are stuck and what is most important for you both to think through together.

The more you use your coaching skills in these one-to-one meetings, the more you will develop them. And hence you will also be more effective when coaching *On-the-Go*, in general situations, with colleagues, bosses and external stakeholders.

Your turn at the controls

If the above descriptions sound different to the norms in your organisation you will need to contract with your team members. They will benefit from understanding what you are trying to do and why – rather than wondering what on earth is happening.

 FLYING STRAIGHT AND LEVEL

1. Put one-to-one meetings in your diary – weekly if possible or less regularly if you think you need more time to help people normalise this type of discussion. The key is the regularity. When you do this:

- Put the meetings in your electronic diary system as repeating events with no end date.

- Explain your aims and ways of working in the first meeting and occasionally repeat this if you think people have not quite got it yet. Acknowledge the aim to have these weekly if you do not start this way. Remember to include an explanation of these meetings to new joiners to the team – consider this a part of their welcome on board (induction).

- Explain that you will commit to keeping this meeting in the diary except in extreme circumstances. Contract with your team member to do the same.

- Agree exactly what those extreme circumstances for cancellation are. Do not be vague. 'If client needs demand it' is far too vague because we should all be managing our time to accommodate client demands. While it's easy to say that clients always come first, if you push that too hard you'll have no staff and then ultimately no clients.

- Follow our guidance in running these one-to-ones.

- If staff members approach you for input or guidance in the time between weekly one-to-ones, first ask if the issue can wait until that meeting. This is important to enable the change in your working styles (if previously you operated on an ad hoc basis), and critically our experience suggests that team members then find their own solutions while waiting.

- Once a month, reflect on the changes in your team since you started these one-to-ones.

- Seek feedback from each team member on how this is going.

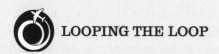 **LOOPING THE LOOP**

This challenge is tougher and will be easier if you have implemented regular one-to-ones with your own team first.

- Approach your boss. Explain the principle of one-to-one weekly meetings. Offer evidence if needed (in addition to this book you will find multiple websites and leadership gurus advocating this approach). Share how it is helping with your own team. And ask to have such meetings with your boss. ▶

- You may find feedback models help you to explain how this arrangement will help you perform more effectively (STARTER™ and SBI models).

- Keep the focus on how this will help you to improve through learning from your boss. And if you have a boss who needs to know what they get out of something too, then address this as well.

Building rapport *On-the-Go*

Quite a few occupations require professionals to learn how to build rapport. Doctors, management advisors, teachers and coaches rely on relationships that feel trusting. Without a bond of trust, people will not reveal their inner thoughts as they simply cannot relax enough to be quiet and reflective. This is why building rapport can be so important.

Usually building rapport is one of the first skills taught in a coaching programme because the baseline of trust is important to establish quickly at the beginning of a new relationship. Otherwise, surprise, surprise, the relationship won't ever grow and develop. However, we urge you to think regularly about rapport and consider whether you have done enough or need to do more to keep the relationship continually alive and developing.

Neurolinguistic programming, also known as NLP, is a method that teaches matching and mirroring. In this approach, you pay attention to the body language of another person and follow their lead in the way you sit and use gestures and verbal language. Although both of us have done some NLP, it is not something that we rely on. Jenny particularly has strong counter-arguments to NLP because in her experience it can lead to a slightly disingenuous mindset. Taken to extremes, it can also feel or seem manipulative and controlling.

Much more helpful, is a genuine wish to understand another person. This means putting aside judgements and cognitive evaluations and instead focusing entirely on the other person and their expressed and unexpressed needs. You will find that quite naturally your demeanour becomes attuned to the other person. It does not require a technique – just to be deeply human.

So instead of watching someone with a view to mirroring or matching them, watch instead in a way so that you are fully absorbed in their experience of the world. Just for now, allow their hardships to be yours and their triumphs to be events that you relish too. There will be plenty of time over the course of the relationship for you to exercise your judgement, but particularly at the beginning suspend your need to evaluate what is happening and instead understand that this is their reality.

This non-judging tuning in to a person will help you to begin to see a much wider set of cues that communicate what they are thinking and feeling, beyond what comes out of their mouth. For example, there are a multitude of muscles in the face that are responsible for micro expressions. These are the small movements that indicate something is happening beneath the surface.

Jenny was once coaching a husband and wife jointly, and noticed a very small facial change in the woman. Jenny asked, 'What's happening for you right now?' and the woman burst into tears. That wasn't the noteworthy event though – it was the husband's question that merits our attention. He asked: 'How did you know? We've been married ten years and I would not have known that anything was going on.' Right. While he cared enormously, he'd stopped watching and really looking.

Your turn at the controls

This activity invites you to find the authentic connection that you can generate with someone, even when you are not entirely agreeing with them. Putting aside the judging and simply connecting is a special skill. See how you get on with the following:

▶

FLYING STRAIGHT AND LEVEL

1. Let's start with in-your-head practices:

- In the next meeting you attend, watch out for micro-expressions. Without judging what those micro-expressions might mean, consider what you might do to help that person in that moment.

- Listen intently for language, use of vocabulary, voice pitch or volume. Without judging what that might mean, consider how you would build or deepen your rapport with that person.

2. At the next social event that you attend where you want a little fun, approach a stranger and practise your rapport-building skills:

- Introduce yourself and remember their name. If it is natural to you, use their name during the conversation.

- Be fascinated by what they are fascinated by.

- Give them your full attention, without sweeping the room with your eyes looking for friends.

- Observe how they use the space around them and hence how close to you and others they feel comfortable with. Adjust your physical proximity to them accordingly. (This use of space will often be culturally distinct so misreading this by standing too close can badly reduce rapport.)

- Do not allow yourself to get bored by the conversation, making it your job to keep the conversation lively.

- After you say goodbye to your new friend, review in your head what you learned.

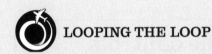 **LOOPING THE LOOP**

This exercise is best practised in informal situations or where you are explicit about what you are trying to do, say in an exercise at the end of a team meeting. Only once you are comfortable doing it should you aim to do this explicitly when coaching *On-the-Go*. Otherwise, you risk reducing the rapport and your coaching effectiveness while your focus moves away from coaching.

1. Notice whether your coachee speaks quickly or slowly, uses long sentences or short ones, uses long words or short words. Then seek to communicate in the same style as they do.

2. Notice if your coachee speaks loudly or quietly, in a low tone or a high tone, calmly or in agitation. Then seek to communicate in the same style as they do.

3. Notice and reflect on what happens as a result.

4. Consider building rapport through the use of visuals or through drawing. For example, you can ask someone to draw a timeline of an event that you are debriefing and have the timeline in front of you to help with the discussion. Or, you might print out one of the models that we present in this book and use it as the focus in a conversation. Or, you might draw a simple diagram of relationships and ask your coachee to amend the diagram (handing them the pen).

THINGS TO DO BEFORE THE NEXT FLIGHT

The ideas behind non-judging are evident in a school of counselling called 'focusing'. We recommend Eugene T Gendlin's *'Focusing: How to Open Up Your Deeper Feelings and Intuition*, published in 1982 by Bantam'.

Watch a video on YouTube by the Centre for Creative Leadership which explains and illustrates the SBI model we provide a link on our website.

For further resources go to: www.coachingonthego.co.uk

Chapter **15**

More about 'IS IT WORKING?'

What impact is your coaching having?

At the start of this book we identified the relatively limited amount of academic, detailed, empirical research there is in the field of coaching. This should not be much of a surprise as it is a relatively new field within leadership. Although it may seem surprising,

it is worth mentioning that the professionalism of management and executive coaching has only reached critical mass in the last 20 years or so. Hence, we are relatively constrained in our ability to analyse and describe the absolute impact that coaching has.

It will always be a challenge, given that coaching happens in the messiness of everyday life *On-the-Go*. Nonetheless, we still consider it vitally important to consider what impact your coaching is having. Both with respect to whether you are moving your coachee forward in their development and solutions, and whether coaching is worth your investment. We will investigate each of these questions and offer practical advice in the usual way – for implementation *On-the-Go*. And we will start with a related and yet critical question: Have you fallen into the trap of *phoney-coaching*?

What is *phoney-coaching*?

Do you remember when you were at school and teachers, either in exasperation or through poor training, asked questions that you knew the answer to even though you had no idea about the content? Perhaps they might emphasise the answer within the question: 'Did Henry VIII reign before or *after* Edward II?' You did not know the facts but you knew the answer because it was signalled to you. You were rewarded for a question you did not actually know the answer to – and you probably would not remember either. This is similar to *phoney-coaching*.

Phoney-coaching occurs when someone is taking a coaching approach and yet wants the coachee to come to a specific answer or outcome. And if they do not reach that answer, the coach will keep asking questions until they do. And then they will stop asking questions relieved that the coachee has finally understood. The problem is that the coachee may not have understood anything more than that this was the outcome you wanted them to reach, rather than the outcome they wanted to reach and to believe in.

Effective coaching is based on the presumption that the way a coachee interprets a challenge and the actions they take to move forward are acceptable. You are supporting them to find their own way. There are exceptions when you must guide them and take off your coaching hat. For example, if a coachee might unintentionally breach an organisational rule. And yet the principle is that the coachee identifies their own journey to self-improvement. Hence, if you have already defined what that journey should be, you are at risk of *phoney-coaching*.

Phoney-coaching quickly comes across as patronising. It fails to change people's behaviour – at least not through choice. Someone who has a habit of taking this approach, like the poorly trained teacher, loses their impact as a role model and motivator. The coachee knows they just need to wait until they guess correctly and then they can move on.

You need to watch out for this trap. The reason it becomes a trap especially for a leader is that you also have a role to inform, advise and guide your colleagues. Sometimes there is a right answer. Not getting budgetary sign-off at the appropriate time can have terrible consequences that must be avoided at all costs (forgive the finance pun). And so there can be a balance to play. In a perfect world such outcomes can be learned through coaching as they will probably have a more lasting effect.

With a junior employee who knows you are helping them to think through their challenges to identify the solution for themselves (good contracting), they can respect that you already know the answer, and you are challenging them to work it out for themselves. Get this wrong, stop when they've reached the right answer rather than exploring all the options first, and you can be both patronising and fail to generate permanent change. Think carefully and consider whether a more directive approach providing feedback might work better.

Your turn at the controls

Just holding the idea of *phoney-coaching* in your head should help to reduce the chances of you falling into this trap. And yet here are a few specific steps to help you raise your awareness and decide what to do if you sense it is happening to you.

 FLYING STRAIGHT AND LEVEL

1. Next time you intend to use a coaching approach ask yourself both what your intentions are and 'Is there a defined answer to this issue that I want my coachee to reach?' If so, is a feedback or directive approach likely to be more effective?

2. If you sense that you are asking a leading question, try to ask it a different way. If you have asked a leading question, have the confidence to acknowledge it: 'I'm sorry I think that might have been a leading question. Please go with it for a second and see if it takes you somewhere useful.'

3. And if you sense that someone is coaching you and has fallen into the *phoney-coaching* trap, we recommend that you call it out. Use naming (see Chapter 6) to explain how you feel, without judging, given that you may be wrong – and ask for their reactions.

 LOOPING THE LOOP

1. Next time you are coaching someone and you suspect you may be leading the outcome (a sure sign of *phoney-coaching*) make sure you debrief with your coachee and have an adult conversation about it. You might say: 'I'm wondering about my coaching style in that conversation because I notice that I held a particular point of view and although I tried to remain completely neutral, did I steer the conversation unnaturally?' By being transparent and sharing the dilemma with your coachee, you demonstrate this is an adult relationship where speaking about underpinning assumptions, feelings, fears and beliefs is helpful.

2. Next time you use your coaching skills *On-the-Go*, check in with yourself afterwards and ask if you accidentally used a *phoney-coaching* style. If so, you will be more prepared next time.

Coaching evaluation - within the coaching journey

In Chapter 10 we explored the importance of helping your coachee design actions to make progress on their topic. A related step is to help your coachee maintain progress by evaluating the activity to date. The regular one-to-one meetings can play an excellent role in this because it is an opportunity to check in.

When you are having a coaching conversation (one that is explicitly identified via contracting that is focused on change and development), you should take the opportunity to check specifically on the actions your coachee and you agreed at the end of the last conversation. Take time to review how those actions turned out in practice. The best time for this is normally at the start of each conversation although time constraints and urgent issues may adjust this. For example, sometimes someone just needs to offload, to complain to a sympathetic ear, so that they can move forward. Otherwise, ask your coachee to share what they said they were going to do in the last conversation and what progress they have made.

This step is not to judge them. It is to help them. It can identify what they find easy to do versus what they find hard. What they can commit to in theory, and yet find immensely difficult in practice. Such issues require exploration to find new ways ahead. In a sense these things are an evaluation of your coaching skills as distinct to the capabilities of the coachee.

When you wear a leader hat as well, it is also an opportunity to praise and draw attention to the coachee's success. Success is often not celebrated but instead is an assumed requirement of the job: 'We expect you to improve and we'll pay you accordingly, so get on with it.' This misses the chance to motivate your coachees. And you can use our feedback techniques to assist here (see STARTER^{TM} and the SBI model).

Coaching evaluation - of the coaching journey overall

Assessing the success of a coaching relationship can become a project in itself, so before reading further, take a little time to decide what is the motivation for this assessment. There are at least three stakeholders who may wish for some assessment, and this to a large extent will help determine what evaluation you undertake:

- **The coachee**: Individuals who have been coached and who continue to be coached will appreciate a sense of progress. Having a sense that things are changing and that personal development is yielding some rewards will keep them motivated and engaged in the coaching endeavour.

- **You, as a coach**: You may want to have some sense that you have made a difference and that the skills you are developing are helping to support other people in their development. Also, you may want some feedback on what it feels like to be coached by you, so that you can continue to improve your skills.

- **The organisation**: Organisations are often keen to measure return on investment (ROI) of coaching assignments. If you are working within an organisation where this is a question, then this drives a whole different set of questions around assessment.

We will address these three, but recognise that there could be other stakeholders or other reasons for wanting to undertake coaching evaluation. However, we're sure that by addressing the above, we can cover most situations.

THE COACHEE ASSESSING THEIR LEARNING

You could do this type of assessment informally. That is, a review conversation about the series of conversations that you've been having. About half-yearly is a good frequency to sit back with your coachee and ask questions about what they have learnt, what they'd like more of or less of from you as a coach, what behavioural experiments have really stayed with them, and how all this work is showing up in their lives?

The focus is on their assessment of the process and their own journey. There's no need to make it too formal or too evaluative. This is about checking that coaching has been helpful and in what way.

ASSESSING YOUR EFFECTIVENESS AS A COACH

If you are new, or even if you have been using a coaching mode of leading for a while, you may be curious to learn how effective you are as a coach, or whether you have developed a few habits. Many coaches ask their coachees to evaluate them at the end of an assignment and this might be appropriate for your situation, but we suspect not.

First, as you are using coaching *On-the-Go* it may be difficult to identify exactly what you have been doing and when you have been doing it, such that your coachee can specifically provide feedback on this.

Second, there might be a conflict of interests especially if your coachee is a direct report of yours.

Third, there is a tendency for coachees to rate their coach as a question of 'satisfaction', but satisfaction is not really the issue. Someone can be highly satisfied with their experience of coaching and it can make no perceptible difference. So, our view is that asking your coachee is nice and respectful, but it is of limited value to you as you grow your coaching skills.

A better way to assess your personal coaching skills is to consider a professional coaching programme or an external coach with the skills to assess your impact (see the Appendix where we discuss the professional bodies that offer these services). At a coaching programme you will have the opportunity to be observed as you coach and to receive helpful feedback in the moment. Nothing improves your coaching as much as peer review and feedback.

THE ORGANISATIONAL REQUIREMENTS TO EVALUATE COACHING

If your organisation has dedicated time and effort to a coaching programme and you are part of it, they will probably have set out in advance how they will evaluate the return on investment. This varies widely between organisations and is largely beyond the scope of this book, designed to assist you as a leader who coaches. Return on investment is measured in a variety of ways, and if this is of interest to you we have provided specific resources for you on this subject at the end of this chapter in the usual way. (And frankly, as researchers and coaches, it is a service that we offer.)

Your turn at the controls

Here's a selection of simple steps to start the self-evaluation process both for you and your coachees.

 FLYING STRAIGHT AND LEVEL

1. As part of the contracting conversation, get agreement about what each of you wants to achieve. Write it down. Review this statement often.
2. Help your coachee to design their own method of collecting feedback.
3. No matter how short your coaching *On-the-Go*, bookend your conversations with the front end looking back and assessing actions from last time, and the back end looking at what will be done after this conversation.

 LOOPING THE LOOP

1. If you're interested in developing as a leader who coaches, consider your own goals and objectives for the year and think about adding something into that aligned to growing the capability of your team or others. In this way, you align your coaching with the performance management system.
2. Align your coaching goals to company goals. Figure out how you might assess the achievement of these goals. Follow through.
3. Consider setting behavioural goals with your coachee. Ask others to help assess whether behaviour has changed. Ensure this behaviour is aligned to company requirements.

THINGS TO DO BEFORE THE NEXT FLIGHT

Read Rebecca Jones, Stephen Woods and Yves Guillaume's 'The effectiveness of workplace coaching: A meta-analysis of learning and performance outcomes from coaching' in *The Journal of Occupational and Organizational Psychology*, pp. 249–277 (2015).

Read AM Grant and MJ Cavanagh's 'Evidence-based coaching: flourishing or languishing?' in *Australian Psychologist*, 42(4), pp. 239–254 (2007).

Read DC Feldman and MJ Lankau's 'Executive coaching: A review and agenda for future research' in *The Journal of Management*, 31(6), pp. 829–848 (2005).

For further resources go to: www.coachingonthego.co.uk

Chapter **16**

More about
PROFESSIONAL
COACHING

How this book has prepared you

There is an ever-growing body of people seeking accreditation for their coaching skills. This can be through university courses as well as through professional bodies. You may be interested in this simply to advance your personal knowledge, to demonstrate your leadership skills to an employer or to become a professional coach.

Whatever the inspiration, here we provide you with an academic understanding of coaching, how the numerous professional bodies identify the underlying skills of coaching and how these link to what you have learned or can learn from our book. Remember that the focus of this book is to enable leaders to have great coaching skills as a leadership capability.

We start by identifying each of the relevant skills and competencies of coaching before offering you our own consolidated view. We do not include any practical activities for you. Some people are interested to understand the background and justification of the skills needed to be an effective coach. If you are one of them, this is for you. Equally, you may find it helpful to clarify these different skills to help you explain and guide others around you in their coaching capability. On the other hand, if you are more interested in the practical day-to-day activities to improve your coaching skills you can skip this.

Below we look at the evidence of some skills having more impact in a coaching situation. This evidence guides our aggregation of the lists produced by the professional organisations. First, we need to introduce the word 'competency' because it is used by all the professional coaching bodies. However, it is used in different ways and some people seem to make an artform out of obscuring the difference between competency and skill.

The online Cambridge Dictionary defines competency as 'an important skill that is needed to do a job' and then lists synonyms such as skill, talent and ability. That's a good-enough definition for our purposes. However, be aware that on other websites there are alleged differences between a competence and a skill. There may be a nuance we haven't yet grasped, so for now let's stick with the Cambridge definition.

Professional coaching bodies

According to an online article in *Forbes Magazine* in 2017 by Connie Whittaker Dunlop of the University of Virginia, there may be around 36 professional coaching associations, most based in the US, but a fair few in Europe, South America and Australasia. These professional bodies are committed to promoting and ensuring good practice in coaching and to help with the self-regulation of the coaching industry. They all make claims as to their importance and impact. And the biggest ones have also started to work together in recent years in an attempt to coordinate and simplify the industry.

International Coaching Federation

Phil is a member of the International Coaching Federation (ICF), founded in 1992 by coaches to provide a professional network for other professional coaches. The ICF recognises different levels of certification, accredits coaching schools, runs yearly conferences around the world, has a list of standards and competencies and a set of ethical guidelines. Although based in the US, the ICF has local chapters all over the world. As one of the well-established and well-recognised coaching bodies, we use its list of competencies as the main criteria we have adopted in this book. The ICF core competencies are:

1. Meeting ethical guidelines and professional standards

2. Establishing the coaching agreement

3. Establishing trust and intimacy with the client

4. Coaching presence

5. Active listening

6. Powerful questioning

7. Direct communication

8. Creating awareness

9. Designing actions

10. Planning and goal setting

11. Managing progress and accountability

Association for Coaching

By way of contrast, Jenny is a member of the Association for Coaching (AC), which aims to inspire and champion coaching excellence. The AC was established in 2002 and is dedicated to promoting best practice and raising awareness and standards of coaching worldwide. It too has a code of ethics and a list of competencies that coaches are expected to train in and continue to develop throughout their career. The AC competencies are:

1. Meeting ethical, legal and professional guidelines

2. Establishing the coaching agreement and outcomes

3. Establishing a trust-based relationship with the client

4. Managing self and maintaining coaching presence

5. Communicating effectively

6. Raising awareness and insight

7. Designing strategies and actions

8. Maintaining forward momentum and evaluation

9. Undertaking continuous coach development

These AC competencies appear to overlap with those of the ICF although they do not match them exactly. And this theme continues as we look at other bodies.

Other international bodies

In addition to the two professional bodies that we belong to, others are worthy of note and inclusion because they offer a non-Anglo-centric view of coaching. The first is the European Mentoring and Coaching Council (EMCC), which aims to develop, promote and set the expectation of best practice in mentoring and coaching across Europe and beyond. It started in 1992 as the European Mentoring Centre (EMC) and has an illustrious list of alumni. Its competencies are once again similar although not identical to those already cited above. Hence to avoid too much repetition these are provided in Appendix A (alongside those of the ICF and AC, repeated for ease of comparison). Similar to the other bodies, the EMCC has a strict ethical code.

In South Africa, Coaches and Mentors of South Africa (COMENSA) is the professional body. It regulates the coaching and mentoring professions in that country through a professional code of ethics and conduct, professional designations, ongoing continuing professional development, professional supervision and access to resources. We could not source a competency framework from this regional body.

The Worldwide Association of Business Coaches (WABC) is based in Canada, and in cooperation with Middlesex University in the UK it also provides a fully accredited Masters degree for experienced business coaches.

All these professional bodies and all these lists of competencies have far more detail which we don't reproduce here and in most cases each competency is developed along a skills continuum, for example, from beginner to advanced to mastery. If you are interested in developing as a coach, we strongly recommend that you consider joining one of these professional bodies and diving into the particular competencies that they value.

However, given that no one professional body can lay claim to a scientific basis for their particular list, although they all look admirable for the purposes of this book we have taken a simple and pragmatic approach. Our rationale is that where a competency, or its near equivalent, is represented in several lists, it is likely to be more central to the coaching role. And where a competency is represented in just one list, while it might have huge value, we cannot validate that and nor does space allow for a full exploration of everything. So with some regret, we have set it to one side.

One further consideration is the evidence from Richard Boyatzis' research (see the suggested reading at the end of the chapter) which we feel must be prioritised in any short list.

We have endeavoured to sort, collate and amalgamate the lists from the four chosen professional bodies to find the most representative core competencies upon which we have relied in the book.

Core competencies

We propose that there are 11 competencies that underpin all coaching. As we've explained, there is no more or less scientific evidence for this list, but it is based on the global professional bodies that we review above and as such we believe it's as good as any around from which to build coaching skills. Our proposed list is:

1. Integrity, and the ethics that guide the coach's actions
2. Knowledge of boundaries including issues of contracting and confidentiality
3. Self-awareness and emotional insight into self
4. Empathy for others
5. Trusting professional relationships
6. Listening to understand
7. Powerful questions
8. Clear communication
9. An ability to promote and support awareness in others
10. Collaborative action planning
11. Cultural and business context sensitivity

While there is a distinct list of competencies here, this is not how skills get used nor is it how they can be taught and learned. This is because it is rare that you might do one thing without accompanying it with another. For example, it is hard to imagine asking questions without listening to the answers you get back. It is for this reason that we have provided a journey through these competencies in Part 2 of this book, which does not start at item 1 and finish at item 11.

So where next?

If you are interested in pursuing professional accreditation, we recommend talking to as many professionally accredited coaches as you can to understand their experiences. Given that most people only ever join and are accredited by one such body, comparisons between them are somewhat challenging. Furthermore, some of the bodies are increasingly seeking to work together to bring consistency to the profession.

The key is to find an introduction and a personal recommendation for an accredited trainer of coaches – a body accredited by one of the professional coaching bodies to train you to become a professional coach. The process is experiential so you are looking for an organisation to train you that you trust.

And another route, which has worked for many people in the past, is to find out if your organisation (assuming you work for one) has its own internal training process for coaches or will fund your coach training. Such a route is extremely helpful given the support this will provide in addition to a willing group of volunteers on whom you can openly practise your coaching skills, a requirement of all the accrediting bodies.

And here's something radical – an elephant in the room if you will. While there is a growing profession of accredited coaches, and so HR professionals are increasingly demanding that external coaches hold such accreditation, there are many highly effective coaches that do not hold any such qualification. This could be an indication of the relative youth of the coaching profession. It is also a reflection of the fact that word-of-mouth references is a critical component of such a personal service. So, depending upon your other professional experience, you may be able to build up a strong coaching business without a coaching qualification.

Assuming you have diligently followed the many exercises and activities in this book, we believe you will be extremely well placed to become an accredited coach. And we hope you enjoy noticing the connections as you go through that process.

THINGS TO DO BEFORE THE NEXT FLIGHT

Read KM Blumberg's 'Executive coaching competencies: a review and critique with implications for coach education' in *The Journal of Psychological Issues in Organizational Culture*, 5(2), pp. 87–97 (2014). ▶

Read Richard Boyatzis' 'Core competencies in coaching others to overcome dysfunctional behavior', in *Linking Emotional Intelligence and Performance*, pp. 81–95 (2013).

Read Richard Boyatzis *et al*.'s 'Examination of the neural substrates activated in memories of experiences with resonant and dissonant leaders' in *Leadership Quarterly*, 23(2), pp. 259–272 (2012).

The Association of Coaching (AC): www.associationforcoaching.com

The International Coach Federation (ICF): www.coachfederation.org

European Mentoring and Coaching Council (EMCC): www.emccouncil.org

Coaches and Mentors of South Africa (COMENSA): www.comensa.org.za

Worldwide Association of Business Coaches (WABC): www.wabccoaches.com

For further resources go to: www.coachingonthego.co.uk

Before you disembark

Some final and uplifting words from us. We began by reflecting at the beginning of this book that leadership and coaching have much in common. Yet we then differentiated specific coaching skills so that they could be looked at in isolation, broken into component parts and made teachable. However, throughout this book you will have noticed our assumption writ large: leaders who are effective incorporate a large number of coaching skills in their everyday relationships.

Effective leaders work along a coaching continuum, whether this is through the use of single skills such as empathy, or multiple combinations of skills such as naming, questioning, summarising and action planning. They use these skills to create direction, alignment and commitment. But in addition to these worthy outcomes, leaders who coach truly believe in developing people so that they flourish in the workplace. There can be no better legacy to leave behind.

Thanks for flying with us.

Appendix

All materials taken from the relevant organisations' websites were current at time of going to press.

Coaching competencies

The Association for Coaching (AC) competencies:

1. Meeting ethical, legal and professional guidelines

2. Establishing the coaching agreement and outcomes

3. Establishing a trust-based relationship with the client

4. Managing self and maintaining coaching presence

5. Communicating effectively

6. Raising awareness and insight

7. Designing strategies and actions

8. Maintaining forward momentum and evaluation

9. Undertaking continuous coach development

European Mentoring and Coaching Council (EMCC) coaching competencies:

1. Understanding self

   - Demonstrates awareness of own values, beliefs and behaviours; recognises how these affect their practice and uses this self-awareness to manage their effectiveness in meeting the client's, and where relevant, the sponsor's objectives.

2. Commitment to self-development

   - Explores and improves the standard of their practice and maintains the reputation of the profession.

3. Managing the contract

   - Establishes and maintains the expectations and boundaries of the mentoring/coaching contract with the client and, where appropriate, with sponsors.

4. Building the relationship

   - Skilfully builds and maintains an effective relationship with the client, and where appropriate, with the sponsor.

5. Enabling insight and learning

   - Works with the client and sponsor to bring about insight and learning.

6. Outcome and action orientation

   - Demonstrates approach and uses the skills in supporting the client to make desired changes.

7. Use of models and techniques

   - Applies models and tools, techniques and ideas beyond the core communication skills in order to bring about insight and learning.

8. Evaluation

   - Gathers information on the effectiveness of own practice and contributes to establishing a culture of evaluation of outcomes.

The International Coach Federation (ICF) core competencies are:

1. Meeting ethical guidelines and professional standards

2. Establishing the coaching agreement

3. Establishing trust and intimacy with the client

4. Coaching presence

5. Active listening

6. Powerful questioning

7. Direct communication

8. Creating awareness

9. Designing actions

10. Planning and goal setting

11. Managing progress and accountability

Worldwide Association of Business Coaches (WABC) coaching competencies:

SELF-MANAGEMENT - KNOWING ONESELF AND SELF-MASTERY

1) Knowing yourself - self-insight and understanding

   a) Having ready access to your thoughts and feelings and being aware of how they affect your behaviour.

2) Acknowledging your strengths and development needs

   a) Having a realistic perception of your strengths and development needs - knowing your strengths and limitations and showing a commitment to continuous learning and self-development.

   b) Self-belief - believing in your self-worth and capabilities.

3) Self-mastery - managing your thoughts, feelings and behaviours in ways that promote behaviour contributing to career and organisation success

a) Self-regulation – managing your reactions and emotions constructively

b) Integrity – choosing ethical courses of action and being steadfast in your principles and beliefs

c) Self-responsibility – assuming personal responsibility and accountability for your performance

d) Adaptability – flexibility in handling change

e) Emphasising excellence – setting for yourself, and confidently pursuing, challenging goals and high standards

f) Initiative – taking independent action to change the direction of events

g) Creativity and innovation – being receptive to new ideas and being able to generate alternative ways to view and define problems

CORE COACHING SKILL-BASE

1) Creating the foundations for business coaching

a) Working within established ethical guidelines and professional standards

b) Agreeing on a clear and effective contract for the coaching relationship

2) Developing the business coaching relationship

a) Establishing trust and respect

b) Establishing rapport

3) Promoting client understanding

a) Listening to understand

b) Questioning effectively

c) Communicating clearly

d) Facilitating depth of understanding

4) Facilitating the personal transformation

   a) Promoting action

   b) Focusing on goals

   c) Building resiliency

   d) Managing termination of coaching

5) Professional development

   a) Maintaining and improving professional skills

BUSINESS AND LEADERSHIP COACHING CAPABILITIES

1) Alignment

   a) Understanding the business and displaying a strong grounding in business knowledge and competencies

   b) Demonstrating proficiency in systems thinking

   c) Aligning coaching initiatives with the business

2) Leadership knowledge and credibility

   a) Acting as a strong and influential role model

   b) Possessing thorough working knowledge of the world of the executive leader and leadership development

   c) Displaying highly developed communication and interpersonal competencies

3) Coach as leader and developer of own business

   a) Creating and managing business relationship networks

   b) Collaborating with other coaches

   c) Developing yourself in a business capacity

4) Creating and maintaining partnerships with all stakeholders in the business coaching process

5) Understanding organisational behaviour and organisational development principles

6) Assessment

   a) Assessing the client

   b) Assessing the individual and organisational benefits of business coaching

7) Having respect for and knowledge about multicultural issues and diversity

Index